D0486584

THROUGH THE YEAR DEVOTIONALS

Courageous Faith
by Bill Hybels

Hearing God
by Dallas Willard

Knowing God
by J. I. Packer

My Heart—Christ's Home
by Robert Boyd Munger and others

Also from InterVarsity Press

Commitment: My Heart—Christ's Home
(Christian Basics Bible Study)

My Heart—Christ's Home
(Booklet)

My Heart—Christ's Home
(Gift Edition)

My Heart—Christ's Home
(Miniature Gift Edition)

My Heart—Christ's Home: 50th Anniversary Edition
(Leather Slimline)

My Heart—Christ's Home Retold for Children
(Hardback Edition)

My Heart—Christ's Home Retold for Children
(Booklet)

MY HEART—CHRIST'S HOME

Through the Year

Robert Boyd Munger
and others

Compiled and edited by
David A. Zimmerman and Cindy Bunch

InterVarsity Press
Downers Grove, Illinois

InterVarsity Press
P.O. Box 1400, Downers Grove, IL 60515-1426
World Wide Web: www.ivpress.com
E-mail: mail@ivpress.com

©2004 by InterVarsity Christian Fellowship/USA. My Heart—Christ's Home ©1954, 1986, 1992 by InterVarsity
Christian Fellowship of the United States of America.

All rights reserved. No part of this book may be reproduced in any form without written permission from InterVarsity Press.

InterVarsity Press® is the book-publishing division of InterVarsity Christian Fellowship/USA®, a student movement active
on campus at hundreds of universities, colleges and schools of nursing in the United States of America, and a member
movement of the International Fellowship of Evangelical Students. For information about local and regional activities, write
Public Relations Dept., InterVarsity Christian Fellowship/USA, 6400 Schroeder Rd., P.O. Box 7895, Madison, WI
53707-7895, or visit the IVCF website at <www.intervarsity.org>.

All Scripture quotations, unless otherwise indicated, are taken from the Holy Bible, New International Version®. NIV®.
Copyright ©1973, 1978, 1984 by International Bible Society. Used by permission of Zondervan Publishing House. All rights
reserved.

Page 328 is adapted from "The Story of a Sermon," originally published in Theology, News and Notes by Fuller
Theological Seminary, March 1979.

Additional permissions are acknowledged on page 329.

Design: Cindy Kiple
Images: Cosmo Condina/Getty Images

ISBN 0-8308-3291-2

Printed in the United States of America ∞

Library of Congress Cataloging-in-Publication Data
Munger, Robert Boyd, 1910-
    My heart—Christ's home through the year / Robert Boyd Munger;
    compiled and edited by David Zimmerman and Cindy Bunch.
        p. cm.—(Through the year devotionals)
    Based on the author's book, My heart—Christ's home.
    ISBN 0-8308-3291-2 (pbk.: alk. paper)
    1. Devotional calendars. I. Zimmerman, David, 1970- II. Bunch,
    Cindy. III. Title. IV. Series.
    BV4812.M86 2004
    242'.2—dc22
                                                                            2004004609

| P | 18 | 17 | 16 | 15 | 14 | 13 | 12 | 11 | 10 | 9 | 8 | 7 | 6 | 5 | 4 | 3 | 2 | 1 |
| Y | 18 | 17 | 16 | 15 | 14 | 13 | 12 | 11 | 10 | 09 | 08 | 07 | 06 | 05 | 04 |

Welcome to my heart—make yourself at home." You can almost picture yourself saying that to Jesus, can't you? It's the impulse behind *My Heart— Christ's Home,* a little booklet by Robert Boyd Munger that for more than fifty years has helped countless people to grasp the idea of surrendering their lives to God. Originally preached as a sermon, the story made its way into several print editions and has inspired much further reflection about the nature of discipleship by succeeding generations of pastors and writers.

In this volume you'll find some of the fruit of Munger's labors. A broad field of Christian writers have lent their voices to the idea of what it would be like to have Jesus as a houseguest. It's our hope you'll find a comfortable spot in your own home to settle in and let their observations and reflections minister to you.

The devotions are organized into weeks that correspond with different spaces in the typical home. For example, in the study we look at how we submit our minds to the lordship of Christ, in the dining room we look at how we control our appetites and desires while feeding our souls, and in the family room (found in the gift edition of *My Heart—Christ's Home*) we experience God's work in our family life. We have also extended Munger's metaphor and added two new rooms: the back porch, which is the place of hospitality, mission and evangelism, and the attic, which is a place for memories. Here and there throughout the devotional you will also find excerpts from *My Heart— Christ's Home.*

Each season of the year takes the reader once through the entire house, from opening the door to Jesus, to transferring the title into his hands. Each week includes six devotions by various contributors, providing a passage from Scripture and a guide toward your own reflection. You may be encouraged to pray, to reflect, to journal, to act. We choose to offer six entries each week rather than seven, assuming that you will use at least one day a week for worshiping God with his gathered people in your church—and also for a built-in bit of grace, as circumstances do sometimes infringe on our devotional time. You might use the seventh day to go back to some of the suggestions at the end of each devotional entry.

The last four weeks of the year are organized for the celebration of Advent. Two days are devoted to each room, so that as you prepare your house for Christmas, you may also prepare your heart for Christ's coming. Other feasts and celebrations remembered on the church calendar are included as well, though the nature of a yearly devotional guide makes perfect alignment from year to year difficult. Holy Week, for example, corresponds roughly to week twelve in the guide. An index of these feasts and holy days is included at the end of this book.

The enduring appeal of *My Heart—Christ's Home* is its promise: When we open our hearts to Jesus, he gladly enters and takes up residence. Munger's description of the experience sets the tone for the devotions that follow: "A deep peace settled down on my soul that has remained. I am his and he is mine forever!"

May Christ settle down and be at home as Lord of your heart also.

Winter

MONDAY

Making Your Heart a Home

> *"Behold, I stand at the door and knock;*
> *if any one hears my voice and opens the door,*
> *I will come in to him and eat with him, and he with me."*

REVELATION 3:20

If you want to know the reality of God and the personal presence of Jesus Christ at the innermost part of your being, simply open wide the door and ask him to come in and be your Savior and Lord.

After Christ entered my heart, in the joy of that new-found relationship, I said to him, "Lord, I want this heart of mine to be yours. I want you to settle down here and be fully at home. I want you to use it as your own. Let me show you around and point out some of the features of the home so that you may be more comfortable. I want you to enjoy our time together." He was glad to come and seemed delighted to be given a place in my ordinary little heart.

REFLECT: *What does it mean for Christ to inhabit an "ordinary little heart"? How do you respond to the idea of giving Jesus a tour of your heart?*

ROBERT BOYD MUNGER

Letting Yourself Be Gathered

> *"How often I have longed to gather your children together,*
> *as a hen gathers her chicks under her wings, but you were not willing."*

MATTHEW 23:37

After a forest fire ravaged Yellowstone National Park, a forest ranger found the charred remains of a bird sitting upright at the base of a tree. When he knocked the bird over, three tiny chicks scurried out from under their dead mother's wings. Because she had been willing to die, the chicks that had been insulated under the cover of her wings would live.

That's the story of the cross. Jesus refused to abandon us. When the blaze of pain wracked his body, he remained steadfast, willing to sacrifice himself so that we could live. Jesus aches for us because he foresees the pain and anguish we will suffer without what he has to offer: new life, everlasting love. He longs to spread his wings over us so that we might live.

JOURNAL: *What are some things in your life you've been unwilling to let Jesus gather together? How can you let Jesus protect you in those things?*

TOM L. EISENMAN

"You call me 'Teacher' and 'Lord,'
and rightly so, for that is what I am."

J O H N   1 3 : 1 3

Jesus was about to be arrested and executed. His disciples were about to betray him, deny him and abandon him. And yet Jesus emphatically declared his lordship: "You call me . . . 'Lord' . . . that is what I am."

Jesus is Lord whether we obey him or not. We sometimes urge people to *make* Jesus Lord of their life, but the fact is that Jesus *is* Lord. We can either live like he is Lord or we can live like we are the ones in charge, but the Bible does not present the fact of his lordship as optional. He called his disciples—and he calls us—to bow our wills to his supreme authority.

Submission to Jesus' lordship doesn't require a religious ceremony or even a church service. Every day, in every decision, in every arena of life, we are to yield to his direction and his authority. "Lordship living" is a lifelong decision that we make every day.

P R A Y : *Acknowledge to the Lord Jesus his absolute authority over you. Willingly submit to his gracious rule in your life.*

DOUGLAS CONNELLY

THURSDAY *The Honored Host*

> *"Zacchaeus, come down immediately.*
> *I must stay at your house today."*

LUKE 19:5

Zacchaeus was not the most honorable man. He was not known for his honesty or his religious fervor. He was the chief publican, a cheat and a crook. He was on Rome's payroll and charged his own people astronomical fees on top of the taxes that the government demanded from them. His neighbors despised him.

Jesus was aware of all of this, yet he made it a point to be a guest in Zacchaeus's home—a home that had been purchased with "stolen" money. Imagine Zacchaeus's amazement: Jesus wanted to spend time with him in his home. He actually invited himself!

And imagine my amazement that although Jesus is fully aware of all my failures, my sin, he wants to move in and make my heart his home. We should rejoice in the fact that Jesus is knocking at the door of our heart. Zacchaeus did not invite Jesus; Jesus invited himself. And you and I didn't choose Jesus first; he chose us. Let's be as responsive, repentant and honored as Zacchaeus was.

ACT: *Thank God that he chose you first. Think of some ways you can express your gratitude to him today through your actions.*

ALEX GEE

Epiphany

> *Magi from the east came to Jerusalem and asked,*
> *"Where is the one who has been born king of the Jews?*
> *We saw his star in the east and have come to worship him."*

MATTHEW 2:1-2

Within days of moving to Atlanta, we made our way to the renowned De-kalb Farmers Market, where we found a vast array of foods—Vietnamese spin-ach, Indian eggplant, Hungarian cheese, Caribbean mangoes, Georgian pea-nuts—under dozens of national flags. The food at the market draws thousands of county residents, originally from over sixty countries, into a multicultural intermingling. Food for the nations!

The church celebrates the Feast of the Epiphany early in the calendar year. We remember the intriguing account of the eastern magi—wise ones—jour-neying to find the infant Jesus and honor him with gifts. Good news had reached the East: Salvation had been made manifest in anticipation of Jesus' call to proclaim his grace to all the world.

If a market draws the international people in our midst, how much more should we who follow Jesus as King draw people from all nations to ourselves?

A C T : *Think of a way to recall the Feast of the Epiphany, traditionally celebrated the first week of January.*

BOBBY GROSS

A Voice and a Dove

*When all the people were being baptized,
Jesus was baptized too. And as he was praying, heaven was opened.*

LUKE 3:21

Crowds of people responded to John the Baptist and his pull-no-punches call to a river-plunge of repentance. So did Jesus. Not because he had patterns of sin to change but because he identified himself with the people—with us— and humbled himself before God. When he came up from the water, dripping and praying, heaven opened. A voice spoke the Father's love, and a dove imparted a holy presence on the scene.

In baptism, whatever its form, we identify ourselves with Jesus and vow to live like him and for him. Today can be an echo of that beginning, a day to change some pattern in our lives that's not good—a spending habit, for example, or an attitude toward a colleague. When we commit to renewal, heaven opens to us. We receive help from God's Spirit and assurance of his love.

REFLECT: *What aspect of your life could you "baptize" today? Pray for God's help and assurance.*

BOBBY GROSS

M O N D A Y

The Study

> *Whatever is true, whatever is noble, whatever is right,*
> *whatever is pure, whatever is lovely, whatever is admirable—*
> *if anything is excellent or praiseworthy—think about such things.*

PHILIPPIANS 4:8

In college my friend Karen and I decided to memorize Philippians 4:8. It proved to be a good way of setting our minds on the things that are above.

When my thoughts are consumed with things that are not true or honorable or pure, I don't seem to have much peace in my life. But how can I think on those things that are excellent if I spend hours filling my mind with what I see on television or surfing the Internet or rifling through magazines? And how will I think on those things that are good if I don't set aside some time to be alone and quiet?

The things we think about influence our actions. When we fill our mind with what is pure and lovely, we will more than likely exhibit the fruit of the Spirit in our lives.

ACT: *Memorize Philippians 4:8, or at least its key words: "true, noble, right, pure, lovely, admirable, excellent, praiseworthy . . . think."*

CAROLYN CARNEY

Smother the Weeds

See to it . . . that no bitter root grows up to cause trouble and defile many.

HEBREWS 12:15

An invasive vine has taken over our front yard and smothered nearly all our plants. We spend hours trying to kill it, yet it continues to come back. Our latest plan is to spread the area with compost and cover it with large sheets of cardboard. On top of that will go another layer of compost. The offending vine will be blocked from finding its way to the surface, and it will die.

As much as I hope this will work, I know I will feel like a murderer as I lay down that cardboard. I'll think, *I'm killing this plant!* I'll admire the glossy green leaves and tell myself the vine isn't so bad after all.

It will take determination to smother that offending growth. I must show no mercy—just as I must show no mercy to resentment or bitter attitudes in myself, even if at the time they appear to be beautiful plants.

PRAY: *Ask the Lord how you can cooperate with him to rid yourself of destructive attitudes that have taken root in your life.*

SANDY LARSEN

Hollow Oaks

See to it that no one takes you captive through hollow and deceptive philosophy.

COLOSSIANS 2:8

In the past couple of years, three large oaks at the edge of our woods have suddenly toppled over. The trees had stood there all my life, and I had thought they would always be there. Each time one of the trees fell we sadly tramped down through the brush to look at the wreck, and each time it was clear why the tree had fallen. The massive trunk was all rotten inside. On the outside the tree had looked healthy, but inside it was hollow.

Our oak trees have outlived several popular trends of thought. Some ideas look sturdy on the outside, but they are hollow, rooted in worldly speculations rather than in God's revealed truth in Scripture. Eventually they will topple like hollow trees.

REFLECT: *When have you trusted in an idea that turned out to be hollow? How can you keep your life firmly rooted in the truth of Christ?*

SANDY LARSEN

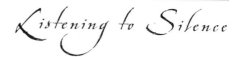

THURSDAY   *Listening to Silence*

In quietness and trust is your strength.

ISAIAH 30:15

I love to study God's Word. I dig into it like digging for a buried treasure. I search for connections and hidden meanings in concordances and commentaries. But as noble as it may be to study the Word, I'm also learning what it means to listen to the space between the words. I often stop and ask, "What's *not* being said?"

It takes both the ink and the page to make a story come alive. In the white spaces of the Bible I discover the silence and emptiness in me. And if I listen to the emptiness, I can make space for God to enter, and I'm undone by the sheer glory of his presence.

The tools of devotion may assist my study of the Word, but it's in the stillness of my heart where I meet the living Word and truly learn to love God.

A C T : *Set aside your normal tools of devotion or your normal routine of study, and ask God to fill in the blank spaces.*

MARSHA CROCKETT

Believing When You Can't See

Faith is being sure of what we hope for and certain of what we do not see.

HEBREWS 11:1

Naomi knew what it was to suffer loss. She called her two daughters-in-law to her and said, "It is more bitter for me than for you, because the Lord's hand has gone out against me" (Ruth 1:13). Uprooted. Completely vulnerable. Not even protected by God. That's how Naomi felt.

When life hits me with a one-two punch I, like Naomi, find it all too easy to lose confidence in the reality of God's protection. "All I know is what I see," I cry out to God, "and what I see is me struggling all alone with no help from you."

Yet the time came when Naomi's friends looked at her newfound security and joy and proclaimed, "Praise be to the LORD, who this day has not left you without a kinsman-redeemer" (Ruth 4:14). God is unchangeable in his goodness, kindness, love, holiness and justice. That is true regardless of how things look to me.

REFLECT: *In what part of God's character do you need to have your faith renewed? In faith, thank him for meeting a need when it still seems hopeless in your eyes.*

KAY MARSHALL STROM

The Mind in Worship

"I am the LORD your God, who brought you out of Egypt."

EXODUS 20:2

In *All Creatures Great and Small*, James Herriot is offered a piece of pie each time he visits a particular farm, and each time he tells the woman of the house that her pies are the most extraordinary in the county. One day she serves him pie as usual. He eats it but says nothing. After a while the woman asks how he liked the pie. He responds, "Well, I'm sorry to say it, ma'am, but the pie is just not up to your usual standards." The woman leaps up and says, "Bless you, Jim!" She had served him a piece of her sister's pie.

The fact that Herriot knew the difference between the woman's pie and her sister's made all of his previous praise even more meaningful to her. In the same way, our God must be pleased when we demonstrate that we know who it is we worship. Our Father looks for intelligent worshipers who know who he is and what he has done, who are discerning in their worship and praise.

JOURNAL: *What are the principal differences between God and the other things in your life that seek your devotion?*

TOM L. EISENMAN

M O N D A Y

The Dining Room

"I have food to eat that you know nothing about."

JOHN 4:32

The dining room—the room of appetites and desires—was a large room in my heart. I spent a lot of time and hard work trying to satisfy all my wants.

I told him, "This is a favorite room. I'm sure you will be pleased with what we serve here: money, academic degrees and stocks, with newspaper articles of fame and fortune as side dishes." These were the things I liked, thoroughly secular fare. There was nothing so very bad in any of them, but it was not really the kind of food which would feed the soul and satisfy true spiritual hunger.

Jesus replied, "If you want food that really satisfies you, do the will of your heavenly Father. Stop striving for your own desires, your own ambitions, your own satisfactions. Put his pleasure before your own. That food will really satisfy you. Try a bit of it!"

And there about the table he gave me a taste of doing God's will. What flavor! There is no food like it in all the world. It alone satisfies. At the end everything else leaves you hungry.

REFLECT: *What's on the menu in the dining room of your desires? What's the recipe for making God's will your soul-satisfying meat and drink?*

ROBERT BOYD MUNGER

*In a large house there are articles not only of gold and silver,
but also of wood and clay; some are for noble purposes and some for ignoble.
If a man cleanses himself from the latter,
he will be an instrument for noble purposes.*

2 TIMOTHY 2:20-21

I wash our cats' food dish, but not as often or as scrupulously as I wash our own dinner plates. The dish doesn't get very dirty because the cats get only dry cat food. Besides, when I watch them lick mud from their own fur, I realize they're immune to things that would make us sick.

On the other hand, our freshly washed dinner plates would not be clean enough for a hospital patient with a life-threatening infection. And NASA would never take our plates into space unless they had been scientifically disinfected.

How clean does a plate have to be? It depends on how it is going to be used. Christ wants clean hearts set apart for him alone. What a blessing that the Master himself is willing to cleanse us and make us pure for his use!

PRAY: *Confess your sins as the Lord reveals them to you, and allow him to cleanse you.*

SANDY LARSEN

WEDNESDAY

What Is Wrong with Me?

My feet had almost slipped; I had nearly lost my foothold.
For I envied the arrogant when I saw the prosperity of the wicked.

PSALM 73:2-3

I am not a naturally content person. I notice people who are more successful than me, or who have more material wealth or appear more at ease in social situations, and I wonder, *What's wrong with me?*

There *are* a lot of things wrong with me, such as bad attitudes and destructive habits. When I look at Christ and compare myself with him, I am painfully aware of my failings. But when I look at other people and demand, "What's wrong with me?" I am not talking about my faults. I am complaining that God hasn't blessed me as much as he has blessed others. Envy leads me to blame God for not being good enough to me. My feet slip off the path of gratitude and I tumble down the hill of discontent.

It is then that I must remember to thank the Lord for all he has given me—only then will I find true contentment.

REFLECT: *Where do you struggle with envy? What can you thank the Lord for right now?*

SANDY LARSEN

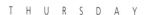

 *Refrigerators*

Then I acknowledged my sin to you and did not cover up my iniquity.

PSALM 32:5

The other night I walked into my friends' kitchen and was surprised to see their old refrigerator in the same place as it had been six weeks earlier—in the middle of the kitchen! They glided around it as if it wasn't even there. When I asked about it they remarked, "Oh, we just don't see it anymore."

How can you *not* see something like that? And yet, there are things that stick out like a sore thumb in my own life that I don't see. I say things to make myself look good, or keep silent when I should speak up, for the sake of my own reputation. But now and again, the Holy Spirit nudges me and I ask for God's mercy and grace.

JOURNAL: *Take a moral and spiritual inventory of your life, acknowledging along the way things that need to be moved or removed. Commit those things to God.*

CAROLYN CARNEY

Harmful If Swallowed

Without wood a fire goes out; without gossip a quarrel dies down. . . .
The words of a gossip are like choice morsels; they go down to a man's inmost parts.

PROVERBS 26:20, 22

I really shouldn't tell you this. . . ."

"Then don't."

That exchange actually took place; I know because I overheard it. Unfortunately, such a conversation is rare.

The proverbs above use two word pictures for gossip. The first says that gossip is like wood for a fire. If you have tended a campfire or a wood stove, you know how a fire dies out without fuel. The second comparison everyone can understand. As we all crave even a bite of our favorite food, so we crave bits of gossip.

To shut off someone who wants to gossip, we don't have to be as abrupt as the person in the conversation above. We can simply respond, "I'd rather you didn't tell me." If the taleteller persists, we can do what we tell children to do with a bully: walk away!

PRAY: *Ask God for the wisdom to know when to shut your ears and when to shut your mouth.*

SANDY LARSEN

A Holy Name

> *On the eighth day, when it was time to circumcise him,*
> *he was named Jesus, the name the angel had given him*
> *before he had been conceived.*

LUKE 2:21

Soon after the start of a new year, we celebrate the Feast of the Holy Name, Jesus. To this name we give our praise, for by it alone we are saved. In it we say our prayers, at the sound of it our knees bow down—as will someday every knee. It is the name above every name, and it is the name we bear if we call ourselves "Christians." So how fitting to pray anew this day, "Hallowed—honored—be your name this year, in my heart and by my life. Help me to live in a manner worthy of your name. Let it guard my soul and govern everything I do or say."

REFLECT: *As you begin the new year in his name, what is one thing in your life that needs to go? One thing that needs to begin?*

BOBBY GROSS

MONDAY *The Living Room*

> *And the peace of God, which transcends all understanding,*
> *will guard your hearts and your minds in Christ Jesus.*

PHILIPPIANS 4:7

It was almost two years after our home burned to the ground before my terminally ill husband and I were finally able to move out of our cramped temporary accommodations and into our rebuilt house. Even after we moved there were workmen everywhere, and my soul longed for a bit of solitude. I yearned for renewal, for respite from my losses.

Only the living room was completely finished, so I carried a chair and a small table over to its sunny corner, and while the workmen sawed and hammered and painted in the rest of the house, I carved out time to feed my soul with God's Word and prayer. How I treasured my time of refreshment! How it lifted my spirit!

Physical rest is healing to the body, but spiritual rest restores the soul. It is only that time of resting in the presence of the Lord that brings us what we long for most: peace that transcends our circumstances.

ACT: *Find a comfortable "living room" space where you can meet regularly with the Lord.*

KAY MARSHALL STROM

Prayer Brings Us to God

Come near to God and he will come near to you.

JAMES 4:8

St. Augustine, the early church father and theologian, said that praying is like a man in a hapless boat throwing a rope at a rock. The rock provides the needed security and stability—life—for the helpless man. Jesus is the rock, and the rope is like prayer, the lifeline that saves the drowning soul.

Prayer is the umbilical cord that provides nourishment to the starving spirit, the channel by which God's life-giving presence flows to us. And it also reminds us that we need God more than he needs us. You see, when the rock is lassoed, the man isn't pulling the rock to the boat (though it may appear that way); the boat is being pulled to the rock. In the same way, prayer is about us moving toward God, not about God coming to us.

PRAY: *While praying, think of yourself in a boat being pulled to shore by your loving Father.*

RICK EZELL

Busy with Life

After he had dismissed them, he went up on a mountainside by himself to pray.

MATTHEW 14:23

When my daughters were little, they loved to play on the neighborhood playground—especially the merry-go-round, where they very quickly acquired a taste for high speed. My job was to be the human piston, pumping the merry-go-round faster and faster until my girls became little more than a blur of squeals and giggles.

One day, in midlap, my youngest daughter decided she was going to hug Daddy on the next pass. The next few moments are difficult for me to recall. My only vivid memory is looking up from the ground, my lip bleeding in two places, and seeing the delighted faces of my two daughters laughing at the raucous good fun we were having.

We learned a lesson that day, and it was simply this: *It's hard to hug a moving target!*

How often do we miss the Father's embrace because we are simply too busy living our lives at a blurred pace of activity and busyness?

ACT: *Set aside time to be alone and be embraced by the love of God.*

DUFFY ROBBINS

But Mary treasured up all these things and pondered them in her heart.

LUKE 2:19

The shepherds left the scene of the infant Jesus' birth and spread the word of what they'd seen far and wide. But Jesus' mother, Mary, had no words to speak of the mysteries that had occurred.

We are often uncomfortable with silence. In conversations, we rush in to break awkward pauses, and in the same way, we often find silence in prayer difficult. We rattle off our shopping list of wants, never listening for what God might want to say to us. And when we do attempt to be quiet, our minds wander, we think of all the things we have to do during the day, and before we know it, our allotted time for prayer has elapsed.

Invariably, we want to fill silence, as if it were empty. But can't silence be full? Think of Mary, who was so full of the precious mystery of Jesus' birth that she dared not speak a word.

PRAY: *Spend at least five minutes a day in silence, listening for God. Try to increase the length of silence in the coming days.*

CAROLYN CARNEY

> *"Be still, and know that I am God."*
>
> PSALM 46:10

How wonderful it is to pray, to take advantage of the privilege of laying my needs and desires before God, of expressing my love and praise to him. It is so good to talk to my Father.

But think for a moment about what we mean when we speak of communication in human terms. It's two-sided, involving both talking and listening. In spiritual terms, prayer is us talking to God, but meditation is God talking to us.

Although prayer is an extremely important part of my quiet time with the Lord, I sometimes wonder if he isn't saying, "You know a lot about me, and that's great. But you don't really know me like you could. Stop talking for a bit and listen."

Some of my most blessed times with the Lord are after I have finished praying and I am sitting in silent meditation. I am still . . . and I know . . . that he is God.

REFLECT: *Read a portion from God's Word; then ask him to guide you as you meditate on it in silence.*

KAY MARSHALL STROM

Restoring Our Souls

*"Come to me, all you who are weary and burdened,
and I will give you rest."*

MATTHEW 11:28

Do you remember the snow days of your childhood? You would get up in the morning and immediately turn on the radio to see if school was going to be closed that day, and when it was, you rejoiced. You had a free day, completely unplanned, in which you could do anything you wanted. It was a gift.

The sabbath is a gift of more than the absence of work; it is a day in which we partake of the wisdom, peace and delight that grow only in the soil of time consecrated specifically for play, refreshment and renewal. Many of us, in our desperate drive to be successful and care for our many responsibilities, feel terribly guilty when we take time to rest. But the sabbath has proven its wisdom over the ages. The sabbath gives us the permission we need to stop, to restore our souls.

ACT : *Block out time on a weekly basis to recharge your soul.*

RICK EZELL

M O N D A Y

The Workroom

> *For we are God's workmanship, created in Christ Jesus to do good works,*
> *which God prepared in advance for us to do.*
>
> EPHESIANS 2:10

I was certain that all of the rooms of my heart remained securely in Christ's possession. Everything was clean, orderly and attractive. I was especially proud of the workroom. People were coming to the Lord through my teaching and publications. I planned prayerfully and carefully, and everything seemed to go as planned.

Then my husband and I had children. We struggled to live out our faith through health crises, school and discipline problems, feelings of inadequacy and pure exhaustion. Of course, there were times of joy and satisfaction too, but parenting is just plain hard work.

Now comes the hard part: trusting God to continue working in the hearts of our adult children now that they are on their own. I have to remember that they are *his* workmanship, not ours.

REFLECT: *What in your life is due to be turned over to the Lord?*

JUDY SHELLY

"My grace is sufficient for you, for my power is made perfect in weakness."

2 CORINTHIANS 12:9

When I began teaching the junior high Sunday school class at our new church, I felt fairly confident. After all, I had taught Sunday school for years. But this class was different. We lurched from Sunday to Sunday, each week holding some novel disaster. One student would storm from the room in anger; another would refuse to come into the room if a certain other student was present. Every Sunday I berated myself because the class didn't realize what a great teacher I was.

Gradually I realized that my confidence was my worst enemy. I had gone into the class with an "I-can-do-this" attitude. I realized that this time I couldn't. I switched my trust from my own competence to the Lord's strength and wisdom, and right away I saw solutions to our problems. While we still have an occasional disastrous Sunday, the class is going much more smoothly—as long as I remember that I have to rely on the Lord, or else!

REFLECT: *Where do you rely too much on your own knowledge? Without belittling your gifts, transfer your full reliance to the Lord.*

SANDY LARSEN

May the Force Be with You

"But you will receive power when the Holy Spirit comes on you."

ACTS 1:8

In the *Star Wars* series of films, Luke Skywalker and other Jedi warriors are locked in a life-and-death struggle with the "dark side" in their attempt to save the galaxy. The warriors have a special calling on their lives, but they are able to fulfill it only through their reliance on "the force," which is always present *with* them and *in* them.

Of course, *Star Wars* is only science fiction, but it beautifully illustrates the spiritual truth of the presence and power of the Holy Spirit in the life of a believer. Just as "the force" is present with the Jedi warriors, the indwelling presence of the Holy Spirit is our constant companion, assisting and empowering us to accomplish the task to which God has called us.

On our own, we are helpless to fight the "dark side." It is only through the power of the Holy Spirit that we can serve God to the fullest.

REFLECT: *Are you attempting to serve the Lord in your own power? If so, confess your failure and begin to rely on his provision as you live out his calling on your life.*

RAYMOND M. CAUSEY

Plug In to the Power

> With great power the apostles continued
> to testify to the resurrection of the Lord Jesus,
> and much grace was upon them all.

ACTS 4:33

The inventor of dynamite, Alfred Nobel, found a way to take a volatile substance, nitroglycerin, and make it stable without diluting its power. The power of God (*dynamis* in the Greek) does the same thing for believers. He makes a volatile life stable by infusing his followers with the capacity to do his powerful work in the world. The same Spirit that gave the early disciples power gives us power.

PRAY: *Ask God to give you power to accomplish his work.*

RICK EZELL

F R I D A Y

I run in the path of your commands,
for you have set my heart free.

PSALM 119:32

God's desires for us are so much bigger and better than the best we can imagine for ourselves. He wants for us nothing less than glory; but we glom on to any number of substitutes for that glory.

Glory poseurs, really—pretenders to the heavenly throne Jesus promised we may share with him in glory. "Popularity?" wrote Victor Hugo, "It's glory's small change." The same can be said of all the other poseurs. Fame? It's glory's small change. Sex? Ambition? Money? Glory's small change.

What do you want out of life: to be a poseur or to occupy a throne? C. S. Lewis suggests that, given the "staggering nature of the rewards promised in the Gospels, it would seem that our Lord finds our desires not too strong, but too weak." God's commands direct us to setting our desires higher, until we are no longer pleased with anything less than glory, and joy inexpressible and glorious.

PRAY: *Pray that God would help you today to discern between the glory he promises us and the substitutes that so often turn our heads.*

BEN PATTERSON

A Good Presentation

When the time of their purification according to the Law of Moses
had been completed, Joseph and Mary took him to Jerusalem to present him to the Lord.

LUKE 2:22

At this time of the year the church recalls the presentation of Jesus in the temple. In keeping with the laws in Leviticus 12, forty days after Jesus' birth Mary presented two doves as a sacrifice in the temple to mark the end of her postpartum "uncleanness." More significantly, in keeping with Exodus 13:2, she and Joseph presented their firstborn as "holy"—set apart, dedicated to the Lord.

Jesus releases us from adherence to the ceremonial law of the Old Covenant but still calls us to the spirit of that law, namely, the giving of ourselves and of our best to God. In Mark 12:30 Jesus placed foremost this command: "Love the Lord your God with all your heart, soul, mind and body" (paraphrase). In keeping with that, we should make a presentation of our "first fruits" every day. We should present our whole selves—our intellectual capacities, vocational talents, financial assets, dearest relationships and more—to the Lord.

REFLECT: *In the spirit of the Presentation of Jesus (traditionally recognized February 2), what is one aspect of yourself that you could present anew to God?*

BOBBY GROSS

MONDAY *The Recreation Room*

Whether you eat or drink or whatever you do, do it all for the glory of God.

1 CORINTHIANS 10:31

We have two rooms in our home devoted to recreation. One contains a TV, a DVD player, a VCR, a computer and an assortment of competitive games. The other room is the garage, where we have the heavier equipment for things like golf, hockey, fishing, camping, baseball, football, bicycling and surfing. Our family takes recreation seriously!

But do all of these things serve the highest purpose—God's—for true recreation? Are these rooms and their toys dedicated to distraction from life or to a part of my overall devotion to honor God in all of my life? What does God want to result from my times of refreshment? When the amusement is over, am I better prepared to serve my Creator with a mindset that is fresh and fixed on him? I need to remember that he is my companion in play as well as work and adjust my perspective accordingly so that I can truly glorify God in all that I do.

ACT: *Consider God's purposes in your next time of recreation, and glorify him with what you do.*

JIM COTÉ

T U E S D A Y

Asking for Help

Carry each other's burdens, and in this way you will fulfill the law of Christ.

GALATIANS 6:2

Rich climbed over piles to reach my office, where I battled deadlines. "Hon, how can I help?" he asked.

Mentally, I took inventory: empty fridge, no dinner planned, piles of laundry, house trashed. Everything in me begged for relief, but instead I performed the "Strong Woman" act. "I'll be okay, Rich. Thanks, though."

His face got sad. "Jane, you don't need me anymore."

Somehow, in the push to be wife, mother, homemaker, writer and speaker, I had swallowed the Great American Lie that I needed to do all things, and needed to do them perfectly. And alone.

Nowhere in Scripture is our aloneness lauded; we were intended to bear one another's burdens, created for relationships, designed for community. My not needing anyone was rooted in pride, and it was killing me, my marriage and my family.

I confess it is still hard to ask for help, but it is a lovely gift I can give to others. They delight in being helpful.

REFLECT: *How is the sin of independence showing up in your life? What small step will you take to overcome it?*

JANE RUBIETTA

Not for Sale

> *"The kingdom of heaven is like treasure hidden in a field.*
> *When a man found it, he hid it again,*
> *and then in his joy went and sold all he had and bought that field."*

MATTHEW 13:44

One of the few TV programs we regularly watch is *Antiques Roadshow*. People bring in all sorts of old objects they have inherited or bought at flea markets or found in dumpsters, and professional appraisers tell them what the things are worth, if anything. One woman brought in her late husband's Gibson guitar. When the appraiser told her that it was worth $40,000, I thought, *What a lucky break for her. That guitar will give her something to live on!* But the woman only smiled and said, "Thank you, but it's not for sale."

When something means the world to you, there is no price great enough to buy it away from you. You have too much joy wrapped up in it. How much is the gospel worth? To the world, not much. To those who find in it their ultimate joy, it is beyond price. They would gladly lose everything else first.

PRAY: *Pray that you will increasingly find joy in the gospel of Christ.*

SANDY LARSEN

THURSDAY   *A Work of Art*

He who began a good work in you will carry it on to completion.

PHILIPPIANS 1:6

Our rec room is filled with arts and crafts. In our family we write and paint and sew and cook and play music in that room.

One of my favorite books on the arts is the devotional by Ken Gire, *The Work of His Hands*. In it Gire considers a slab of marble as a symbol of a life hidden and unformed before God, who chisels away the "self" in order to reveal the inner being—or perhaps his own image inside of that life—in much the same way that I make something out of the tools and materials in our rec room.

As I reflected on these thoughts, I prayed, "Make me unflinching as you chisel out all that is not from you, all that I've used to hide Christ in me. Strip it away with hammer and awl, for I long to be your work of art."

REFLECT: *How is God working in your life to conform you to the image of Christ?*

MARSHA CROCKETT

The master of the banquet tasted the water that had been turned into wine. . . .
Then he called the bridegroom aside and said, ". . . You have saved the best till now."

JOHN 2:9-10

One night during our prayer time before bed, my son asked, "Mom, can Jesus just play soccer with me?"

Quick, think of something theologically sound! "Yes," I said, "Jesus *could* play soccer with you." I imagined Jesus and my son cavorting in the backyard, kicking and dribbling seamlessly and without cheating. Cool.

Jesus went to lots of parties, so he must have known how to have fun. How often I focus my time with Jesus not on enjoying him but on my own stuff: sin, insecurity, complaining, frustration. Jesus died, but he also lived. He was acquainted with sorrow and grief, but he also made wine from water and told parables about banquets.

REFLECT: *Watch some children playing today. Ask Jesus to help you enjoy his presence in your life.*

ALISON SIEWERT

Don't Hate the Player

I went about mourning as though for my friend. . . .
But when I stumbled, they gathered in glee.

PSALM 35:14-15

If you think you've faced humiliation, try playing a video game against an eight-year-old. You'll be killed, reset and killed again, ad nauseam, while a child with no apparent respect for his elders points at you and cackles.

Competition is a core value in free-market cultures. Often competition brings out the best in us: we push each other to excel by testing our abilities against one another. But too often competition brings out the worst in us. We find ourselves wishing that an eight-year-old would fall off his hovercraft into the crater we've created with our laser cannon, or spreading rumors about people in our church who have built a better rapport with the pastor than we have.

It's okay to compete, but eventually all our games will end. It would be a shame if our lust for dominance left us with no one to help us celebrate our victories.

REFLECT: *Who in your life do you feel the most sense of competition with? What can you do to protect your relationship?*

DAVID A. ZIMMERMAN

M O N D A Y

The Bedroom

> *The body is not meant for sexual immorality, but for the Lord,*
> *and the Lord for the body.*

1 CORINTHIANS 6:13

One day when we were in my bedroom Jesus asked me, "You are beginning to question my teaching on sex, aren't you? You're afraid my will on this will limit the full enjoyment of life and love."

"Yes," I confessed.

"Then listen carefully," he continued. "I forbid adultery and nonmarital sex not because sex is bad but because it is good. Beyond physical ecstasy, it is a means of bonding two lives. It has the creative power to bring human life into being. Used properly, sex has tremendous potential for good. Used improperly, it destroys the good. For this reason God intends it to be expressed only within the commitment of a loving life partnership. There is far more to love than just sex."

REFLECT: *How have cultural factors shaped your understanding of the power and potential of sex? How can you trust Christ with your sexuality?*

ROBERT BOYD MUNGER

Belonging to One Another

The wife's body does not belong to her alone but also to her husband.
In the same way, the husband's body does not belong to him alone but also to his wife.

1 CORINTHIANS 7:4

Husband and wife belong to one another in such a way that both desire to please the other as though they were pleasing themselves.

In our age of endless struggle for independence, and in the wake of so many stories of domestic violence and abuse, Christians struggle to find the right interpretation for biblical teachings on marriage relationships. Some come up unduly harsh, and others are watered down to fit our society's current mores. But Paul doesn't need any help. His statement here is straightforward and clear. Writing in an age when it would have been easy to stop after the first sentence of this verse, thereby leaving all the power in the hands of the husband, the apostle adds, "And, wives, it is true for you too."

REFLECT: *In what ways are you pursuing your independence to the detriment of your relationships?*

KAY MARSHALL STROM

Free to Dream

> *"Enlarge the place of your tent, stretch your tent curtains wide,*
> *do not hold back; lengthen your cords, strengthen your stakes."*

ISAIAH 54:2

It's always been easier for me to see the minuses than the pluses, especially in being single. But I've learned a lot from the allegory of the barren woman in Isaiah 54. She is set free to dream, to not be confined, to not define herself by the standards of her surrounding community. The more I thought on this, the more I saw the opportunities I've had in being single. I've had freedom to travel and visit friends around the world and the ability to establish and nurture many intimate, lasting friendships with both men and women. It has provided the availability for ministry. I have been able to relocate, fairly unhindered, to a foreign country, to spontaneously accept an invitation for an evening out or a weekend away, to extend hospitality to visitors.

Though the barren woman may have been marginalized by society, there is much that she can offer. Just like anybody.

JOURNAL: *List the ways God can be glorified by singles. Pray for the singles in your life to glorify God in their singleness.*

CAROLYN CARNEY

Unusual Kindness

Love is kind.

1 CORINTHIANS 13:4

Kindness is one of the qualities of love highlighted in 1 Corinthians 13. On my honeymoon I experienced the immense power of unusual kindness. I stepped out of the shower and began to blow-dry my hair and put on makeup. As I looked in the mirror, I began to critique my twenty-year-old frame. Bill was sitting on the bed listening, and he thought, *Hey, she's criticizing my wife! I could do better than that mirror.* He got up and took my face in his hands. He said, "Pam, if you need to know how beautiful you are, what an awesome woman of God you are, you come see me. I will be your mirror. And if I have to break every mirror in the house to get you to believe me, I will. From now on, Pam, please let me be your mirror." Love is kind.

A C T : *Be a mirror today for someone who is seeing only the worst of who they are.*

PAM FARREL

F R I D A Y   *Feed Me!*

> *Husbands ought to love their wives as their own bodies. . . .*
> *After all, no one ever hated his own body, but he feeds and cares for it.*

E P H E S I A N S   5 : 2 8 - 2 9

Teaching at a high school is tough at any time of the day, but the class period just before lunch is the worst. Food aromas from the cafeteria roll down halls and up stairwells and into eager noses. All the students can think about is food.

Nobody has to tell us to eat when we're hungry. We would not think of starting a long car trip without food or money to buy food. Even for a short hike we may grab some fruit or a candy bar just in case we get hungry. In the Scripture, husbands are told to care for their wives just as diligently and naturally as they feed their own bodies. Surely the advice works both ways. Wives are to care for their husbands just as they feed themselves. We are called to give practical attention to our partner's needs, both physical and emotional. Just as we regularly feed our bodies, we must remember to care for one another.

R E F L E C T : *Is there something you could be doing to tend to the needs of a loved one today? What would it take for you to do it?*

SANDY LARSEN

More Than Enough Love

Love is as strong as death.

SONG OF SONGS 8:6

After three years of trying to have a baby with no success, my wife and I consulted an infertility doctor. Preliminary tests revealed no reason why we couldn't get pregnant. Our doctor said to my wife, "You might have deeper issues that we can explore if you consent to surgery."

We ignored the recommendation and tried for two more years, with nothing to show for our efforts but mounting disappointment and frustration. I started prodding my wife to have the surgery. I'll never forget her retort: "I want to have a child, but I'm not willing to let someone cut me open simply to look around. I'm sorry, but I'm not about to have surgery for someone else, not even you."

I had promised to love my wife as Christ loved the church, giving himself up for her. I realized that my need to be a father was causing my wife to feel like a failure. My dreams had to give way to my sacred vow to be the husband Jesus had called me to be.

REFLECT: *How do your dreams affect your capacity to love another person?*

KEN FONG

M O N D A Y *The Hall Closet*

> *You have set our iniquities before you,*
> *our secret sins in the light of your presence.*

PSALM 90:8

A few years ago my husband and I moved into the house where I grew up. All my parents' belongings were still there. In order to hang up our own clothes, we cleared out the front parts of the closets, but the high shelves and the backs of the closets have taken longer to clean out.

What is so daunting about clearing out a closet? I think it is because few closets have decent lighting or even any light at all. So we work in the dark, always a little nervous about what we'll encounter.

It is often only urgency that prompts a major closet clean-out. When something is missing we have to find it—now. Then we drag everything into the light. In the same way, the Lord is always on an urgent mission to clear sin from our lives. He turns the light of his presence on our secret sins, not to disgrace us but to offer us his grace.

REFLECT: *Where would you prefer to hide from the light of God? Decide now to accept his grace in those areas.*

SANDY LARSEN

T U E S D A Y

Rid Yourself of Malice

Therefore, rid yourselves of all malice and all deceit.

1 PETER 2:1

Malice is an ugly word. It's worse than anger. It has the connotation of intent to harm. I don't want to look at my heart with that in mind. Surely nothing so insidious lurks within. But my petty, hurtful words of yesterday quickly resound: I made sure a family member knew my disappointment when he didn't get something quite right.

Immediately I want to justify myself, but the truth stands: I wanted that person to feel bad for inconveniencing me, for not measuring up. My heart hurts to think of the stream of words that spilled out with malice, an intent to harm. All I can do, as God obliterates my self-righteousness with brokenness, is seek forgiveness from God and from my loved ones and invite the Lord to clamp a guard over my mouth, that I might speak words that edify.

PRAY: *Ask God where malice might hide within your heart, hurting both you and others. What action does he want you to take?*

JANE RUBIETTA

A Cure for Insomnia

"In your anger do not sin":
Do not let the sun go down while you are still angry.

EPHESIANS 4:26

On a recent speaking trip, night after night I tossed and turned. Dogs barked. My roommate snored. Inane songs ran through my mind. I couldn't pray. Fatigue drooped my face. Finally, my good friend and roommate said, "Jane, if I were awake that much, I'd be asking God to show me my sin."

I was horrified, but the gripping of my heart seemed to indicate God's nudging. Skipping the next session, I stayed in my room, journaling. Out poured anger—dark, sludgelike, poisonous. As I dug with the pen, anger at God sprawled over the page for what felt like abandonment. For several years we'd been trying to obey God with our gifts, and every month we barely squeaked by. I wasn't sure he had our good at heart even though I knew he'd called us to this ministry.

My writing turned to tears and confession. Though the pain didn't disappear, God's reassurance and presence came near. And that night, I slept without stirring.

JOURNAL: *When does your anger turn to sin? How can anger direct you to your heart and to God?*

JANE RUBIETTA

Getting Comfortable with Sin

Nothing in all creation is hidden from God's sight.
Everything is uncovered and laid bare before the eyes
of him to whom we must give account.

· HEBREWS 4:13

I make it my policy to never lift up the cushions on our sofa. Before this policy was in place, I once made the mistake of looking for a pen under those cushions. What I discovered was a nightmare of leftover cookies, popcorn, used tissues, a smashed doughnut and the wise man we'd been missing from our nativity scene for three Christmases. And I was faced with the unhappy prospect of having to clean up the mess.

It has been said that the Bible will keep you from sin, or sin will keep you from the Bible. It's true. Scripture exposes the underneath places of our lives, those places we would rather not see, and exposed sin requires that we allow Christ to clean up the mess. That's not always easy, especially if we've become comfortable with our disobedience.

REFLECT: *Do you find yourself unwilling to expose yourself to the probing light of God's Word? Perhaps it is for fear of what you might discover.*

DUFFY ROBBINS

FRIDAY

When I kept silent, my bones wasted away through my groaning all day long.

PSALM 32:3

They're only three little words, a brief sentiment, but they pack enormous power. Even before they are spoken they can lead a grown man to cry. Courage is mustered up, words stumble from your lips, and your heart anxiously beats as you wait for a positive reply. "Please forgive me."

When we do not come clean from sin it has a way of controlling us. We don't laugh easily; we may get headaches or have insomnia. Our relationships can be affected, and we may be filled with resentment, which can boil over into bitterness.

Forgiveness is not a "given" in our human relationships, but we find freedom when we ask for it—whether from God or from others. The onus of granting forgiveness lies with the one who has been wronged. Fortunately, we have a loving Father who longs for our restoration. Those three little words have the power to heal our brokenness.

REFLECT: *Take time to identify any unconfessed sin in your life. Is there anyone with whom you are not at peace?*

CAROLYN CARNEY

Your iniquities have separated you from your God;
your sins have hidden his face from you.

ISAIAH 59:2

Not too long ago God seemed so far away from me. I prayed, read my Bible and went to church, but I felt nothing. Why did God seem to elude me? How could he let me sacrifice all my efforts to come into his presence and yet never seem to show up?

Eventually I heard God's voice. His message was undeniably clear: "Rick, I'm not hiding from you. You've been hiding from me. And before you can come into my presence and enjoy fellowship with me, you must uncover the secrets of your heart and confess the sins of your past."

His words pierced my heart. They were true. I had tried to cover up my sinful secrets. Rather than admit my sin, I had hoped that my spiritual activities of praying, Bible reading and going to church would cancel it out. Or at least that God would overlook my sin because I was being so "spiritual." It did not. And he would not.

PRAY: *It's time to be honest with God. If we want to engage God's presence we must confess our sin.*

RICK EZELL

M O N D A Y

 The Family Room

> *God sets the lonely in families.*
>
> PSALM 68:6

A dear friend and I just spent a day together. She showed me a book she has been reading, and we read passages out loud to each other. We went to dinner together and shared our entrées because we couldn't decide what to order. I asked her advice about a difficult situation and she shared her gentle wisdom. That's how it always is when we're together.

We're family, my friend and I. She has no other family, and she entered my life at a time when my children were away at school, my first husband was at the end of his life, and I was at the end of my endurance.

Have you ever noticed how God has a way of bringing people into our lives just when we need them most? It isn't just by chance, you know. God gently bears those who experience extreme loneliness; then he plucks up others of his people and knits them together into God-made families.

PRAY: *If you are lonely, ask God to provide a family for you. Consider, too, if he might be asking you to be someone else's family.*

KAY MARSHALL STROM

Commit to Authenticity

> *We loved you so much that we were delighted to share with you*
> *not only the gospel of God but our lives as well,*
> *because you had become so dear to us.*

1 THESSALONIANS 2:8

Reuben Gornitzke said, "We can't simply cheer people on and give them our best wishes. We have to make room for them in our lives." It is not enough to admit that we need each other or to say, "Oh, a few friends would be nice." We must get beneath the surface talk and become interested and accountable to each other.

Authenticity occurs when masks come off, conversations get deep, hearts get vulnerable, lives are shared, accountability is invited and tenderness flows. It is when we make room for others in our lives that the walls of indifference and apathy come down. It is when we make room for others that we discover the best in them and the best in ourselves.

We need to take off our masks, admit our need for each other, cultivate relationships and strive for authenticity.

JOURNAL: *What are some of the masks you wear in your relationships? What would it take for you to feel safe enough to shed those masks?*

RICK EZELL

> *"Lend to them without expecting to get anything back.*
> *Then your reward will be great."*

LUKE 6:35

At the age of eleven I was the youngest of three children. I had everyone to care for me and no one to care for. I was, at the time, very happy with that arrangement. However, when my parents began bringing in foster children and placing their cribs in my room, that changed forever. A new feeling of responsibility came with sharing my heart with the tiny brothers and sisters who came into our home.

Opening myself to those helpless ones provided me joy that I could never have anticipated. When we follow Christ's request to welcome, as children do, those who need our love, the reward we receive is beyond what we could have imagined.

ACT: *Identify someone on the periphery of your life who could use a warm welcome. Invite them into your life.*

GREG MYRA

THURSDAY *The Hands of Jesus*

Carry each other's burdens,
and in this way you will fulfill the law of Christ.

GALATIANS 6:2

During my mother's illness, to relieve her itchy scalp, I soaked cotton balls with witch hazel and smoothed them over her head, removing the dead skin. She would coo with delight at the relief of this small annoyance in the sea of all her larger troubles. It was one small way that I could show my love to her with my hands.

Have you ever paid attention to Jesus' hands in the Gospels? You can see them reaching out and touching the leper, making mud and placing it on the eyes of the blind man and taking Jairus's daughter by the hand and lifting her up. His hands embraced children when they came to him, washed dirty feet, broke bread and made breakfast on the beach for the disciples. And, of course, his hands were pierced by nails that were meant for us. We can also use our hands to practically care for someone, to show compassion or offer hospitality.

A C T : *Offer your hands this week to serve someone in need.*

CAROLYN CARNEY

FRIDAY   *Do Not Fail to Pray*

"Far be it from me that I should sin against the LORD by failing to pray for you."

1 SAMUEL 12:23

The phone rang as I was stepping out of the shower. When I picked up the phone, my sister greeted me long-distance. "How are you?" I asked, worried at her workday call.

"Oh, fine." She burst into tears. "I miss you."

We cried together on the phone. Her stepdaughter's wedding that evening was on my calendar, but I hadn't thought of it recently, hadn't invited God to show me how to pray for the people and events involved.

"Are you dressed yet?" I asked, sniffling.

"I have my makeup on but not my dress." More tears.

"Crud, do you have your mascara on already?" I asked.

Sara spurted with laughter, and the sun shone through the rain. When we hung up, I asked for forgiveness for my unceasingly fast-paced life, which leads to thoughtless living. Then I prayed earnestly for my sister and her family for the rest of the evening.

PRAY: *Sit before God with your calendar. Invite him to lead you in prayer for the people and events in your life.*

JANE RUBIETTA

Rejoice with Those Who Rejoice

Rejoice with those who rejoice; mourn with those who mourn.

ROMANS 12:15

The closer the wedding day got, the madder I became. I thought my father was remarrying a bit too soon after my mother's death. Our family had barely cleared her things out of the house when he started seeing someone new. How could he be so inconsiderate of the family's feelings?

Resentment was eating me up. Not only did I resent what my father was doing, I wrote off my future stepmother altogether. I could barely pray except to justify my feelings to God. Eventually, my guilt caught up with me, and I felt remorse for my own selfishness. I did not have much faith, but I asked God to make me truly happy for my father. Why should he have to stay alone?

Coming out of the church on his wedding day, I was surprised by the joy I felt for my father. This was not happiness that I manufactured myself; God had given me a gift.

JOURNAL: *Are you rejoicing, mourning or doing something in between today? How can you prepare yourself to join with people who are feeling differently today?*

CAROLYN CARNEY

MONDAY

The Back Porch

> *"If we walk in the light, as he is the light,*
> *we have fellowship with one another."*
>
> 1 JOHN 1:7

At its beginning love can be self-centered and exclusive. There was a story that made the news about two college kids who disappeared. Turns out that they were in love and ran off to be married. They didn't let family or friends know where they were because they just wanted to be alone together. But eventually they returned and apologized. They discovered that they needed community. Mature love is other-centered and inclusive.

As we bring Christ into every room of our hearts, we experience growth, and we nurture our relationship with Jesus. At the same time we will find that the love growing within us wants to extend outward. At this point we may begin to spend time on the back porch—a place of welcome where we draw others in to our relationship with Christ. By our example and testimony others will be drawn to Christ, finding their own relationship of love with him and with the whole community of believers.

REFLECT: *How could you nurture a few back-porch relationships (with either seekers or believers) that center on Jesus?*

CINDY BUNCH

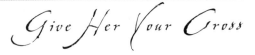

Give Her Your Cross

Through him we both have access to the Father by one Spirit.

EPHESIANS 2:18

A friend once told me, "Jane, I dreamt about you last night and woke up crying. I asked God what to do. He said, 'Give her your cross. She needs it more than you do.'" This woman's son had made crosses out of soldered nails as gifts. Since his death from AIDS, she had had not taken off the cross he made for her.

God was able to turn that woman's suffering into a gift of compassion and intercession. When she draped her cross around my neck, she was symbolizing the bridge that Christ is, redeeming earth's pain and giving us heaven.

Through the cross, Jesus grants us access to the love of God. As we endure suffering, our crosses become opportunities for him to do the same for others.

REFLECT: *What cross can you turn into an opportunity to touch someone else's life?*

JANE RUBIETTA

W E D N E S D A Y

Evidence of Salvation

> *In everything set . . . an example by doing what is good.*
> *In your teaching show integrity, seriousness and soundness of speech*
> *that cannot be condemned.*

TITUS 2:7-8

Three times in Titus 2:1-10 Paul highlights his concern about the effect of the Christian witness on the non-Christian world. In two of those instances he refers to Christian doctrine, which is salvation doctrine. Either we give no evidence of salvation in our lives, in which case the gospel is tarnished, or we give good evidence of salvation by living a manifestly saved life, in which case the gospel shines. Our lives can bring either adornment or discredit to the gospel. The choice is ours each day.

REFLECT: *How could your life more effectively draw seekers to the gospel and to our Savior?*

JOHN STOTT

Get Found!

> *"I have called you friends,*
> *for everything that I learned from my Father I have made known to you."*
>
> JOHN 15:15

Robert Fulghum, in *All I Really Need to Know I Learned in Kindergarten*, writes about sitting in his office and listening to the neighborhood kids playing hide-and-seek. As he wrote, Fulghum noticed a kid under a pile of leaves in the yard just under his window. The boy had been there a long time; everybody else had been found and they were about to give up on him. So Fulghum yelled out the window, "Get found, kid!" He scared the boy so badly that he started crying and ran home to tell his mother. Fulghum says, "It's hard to know how to be helpful sometimes."

We have become a society that plays an adult version of hide-and-seek, and many of us hide too well. Sometimes the best thing that can happen to us is to be found by the people around us, no matter how scary that thought is to us.

A C T : *Who can you risk letting find you today?*

RICK EZELL

Living in Harmony

May the God who gives endurance and encouragement
give you a spirit of unity among yourselves as you follow Christ Jesus,
so that with one heart and mouth you may glorify
the God and Father of our Lord Jesus Christ.

ROMANS 15:5-6

Ten times in the book of Acts, Luke describes a group of people focused passionately on a single purpose with the Greek word *homothumadon,* which comes from two words meaning "unanimity" and "passion."

Paul uses the same word only once, in Romans 15:6, to describe how a common devotion to Jesus brings glory to God. This theme, which reflects Jesus' prayer for his followers in John 17:20-23, is frequent in Paul's letters as well. But nowhere does Paul use stronger language than in this passage about the nature of our "togetherness" in Jesus. Our togetherness is a gift from God that serves as a gift to God.

REFLECT: *What could you do to encourage togetherness in your church? your family? your community?*

STEVE HAYNER

The Announcement

Then Mary said, "Here am I, the servant of the Lord;
let it be with me according to your word."

LUKE 1:38 NRSV

Each year the church reflects on the Annunciation, that is, the announcement by an angel to a young woman of Nazareth that, though a virgin, she would conceive and bear a child to be called the Son of God. Already startled by this being before her, Mary struggles to grasp the message: "How can this be?" The angel asserts a mystery—"The power of the Most High will overshadow you"—and offers a reassurance—"Your old and barren Aunt Elizabeth is six months pregnant" (see Luke 1:35-36). Nothing is impossible with God.

What do you say when God chooses you to step out of your privacy into some momentous task or chooses for you some tumultuous experience? Mary teaches us. However unsettled, we submit ourselves as servants to our Lord. However perplexed, we entrust ourselves to God's plan and purpose. Like her, we say our humble amen: "let it be so."

REFLECT: *What might the Lord be asking you to do outside of your everyday life? What would it take for you to extend yourself if you were called?*

BOBBY GROSS

M O N D A Y

The Attic

> *His compassions never fail. They are new every morning;*
> *great is your faithfulness.*

LAMENTATIONS 3:22-23

When I struggle for a reason to hope, my mind goes to the weeping prophet Jeremiah. How unimaginably horrific it must have been to actually witness the horrors of the Babylonian invasion of Jerusalem. And then to watch as the great temple of Solomon was reduced to rubble! As the people struggled just to survive amid the awful suffering and starvation that followed, the heartbroken prophet picked up his pen and wrote, "Because of the LORD's great love we are not consumed, for his compassions never fail."

How could Jeremiah, surrounded by such horrible suffering and destruction, make such a statement? For only one reason: he knew all about God's faithfulness. He had already experienced it.

Jeremiah reminds me to consider the ways in which God has so often proven his faithfulness to me, over and over and over again.

JOURNAL: *Invite Jesus into the attic of your memory. Think back to the times when God has proven his faithfulness to you, then write them down. When things are at their worst, you can pull out your list and see the proof of God's faithfulness in your life.*

KAY MARSHALL STROM

Transitions

> *[Jesus] said to his disciples, "Let us go over to the other side. . . .*
> *Why are you so afraid? Do you still have no faith?"*

MARK 4 : 3 5 , 4 0

Most of us like stability. Change doesn't come easily, and fear often overtakes us while we're in the midst of a transition: after we've graduated and before we get a job offer; after we get bad news about a loved one and before we hear from him again; after an argument with our significant other and before we make up. In times of transition, the old familiar things have been stripped away and we're left not knowing quite where we are.

It is often during such "in-between" times that God teaches us a life lesson. Transitions can be for us a time of testing to see where our faith is based: Is it on the familiar ground beneath us? in the allure of greener grass on the other side? or in the God who promises to bring us there safely?

JOURNAL: *How has God met you in previous transitions in your life?*

CAROLYN CARNEY

"Teacher, don't you care if we drown?"

MARK 4:38

I had wrestled for years with a tragic drowning that had occurred on a missions trip. I felt abandoned by God; I wondered if Jesus really cared. Certainly, he could have done something that day to alter our situation. We had prayed fervently, yet he had done nothing.

I revisited Costa Rica fourteen years after Nadeene's drowning and met up with three others who had been affected by the tragedy. We'd not seen or heard from one another during all the time that had passed. We talked about how we had wrestled to figure out God's care and goodness, and how we now view suffering and pain.

Jesus hadn't changed our situation that day—he had changed *us*! Jesus had used the tragedy to mold and shape us into the people he wanted us to be. Death is still a mystery to me, but working through tragedy has given me a new perspective on Jesus' care.

REFLECT: *What trials have you experienced lately? How might Jesus use them as a means of shaping you into a more complete person of faith?*

CAROLYN CARNEY

Seeing God in the Rearview Mirror

"Then I will remove my hand and you will see my back;
but my face must not be seen."

EXODUS 33:23

Sort of like looking in the rearview mirrors of our life, it is often only after the fact that we see how God has performed his work. We reflect on an unfolding series of events and know that those pieces could have come together only by the hand of God. We look back at things that happen to us so undeserved and unmerited, and realize that it was God working in our life.

In this Scripture Moses stood in the crevice of the rock, and when God passed by, Moses saw him—not his face, but his back. We too, when led by God, most often do not see God's face, but his back. We do not anticipate God's movement; it is only after long reflection that we are finally struck with what God has been doing all along.

JOURNAL: *Look back on your life. How has God led you? What signs can you see of his touch on your life?*

RICK EZELL

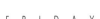

Treasures in the Heart

Mary treasured up all these things and pondered them in her heart.

LUKE 2:19

Early in our marriage we had an invitation to minister in Sweden. We started to write a letter to say that we would come if our hosts provided transportation and financial support for us, but the letter didn't feel right. After praying about it, we decided to go to Sweden and to never tell anyone of our financial need.

Through the next two years God consistently provided for our needs. There were memorable days when we spent the last coin and ate the last of the food in the house. But then God was there with more—and the help never arrived the way we expected; it was always through an unpredictable source.

Time and again we have relied on our experiences in Europe to renew our confidence in God. He was faithful, and he continues to be faithful. Like Mary, we consider what we have seen and ponder its lessons.

REFLECT: *Search your heart for the treasures of remembered blessings, especially when the Lord has come to your aid in surprising ways.*

SANDY LARSEN

Behold Your King

Some of the Pharisees in the crowd said to Jesus,
"Teacher, rebuke your disciples!"
"I tell you," he replied, "if they keep quiet, the stones will cry out."

LUKE 19:39-40

Jesus entered Jerusalem during the last week of his life acclaimed a king. His followers exulted with joy, the crowds stirred with curiosity, and the leaders chafed with resentment. It was to prove a dramatic—and holy—week. Jesus would weep with compassion over his city which, by week's end, would witness his execution.

Our congregation in New York City remembered Palm Sunday by circling our block with palms, singing. We drew puzzled stares and caught-off-guard smiles and, sometimes, genuine interest. In so doing, we reaffirmed our commitment to announcing our true leader to our city. No question, Jesus will have his witnesses. If we don't do it, the very asphalt will sing his praises.

A C T : *As Holy Week approaches and the story of Jesus surfaces in public consciousness, look for a chance to speak to someone about Jesus. Don't be silent.*

BOBBY GROSS

MONDAY

Transferring the Title

This is what I seek:
that I may dwell in the house of the LORD all the days of my life.

PSALM 27:4

I try to keep my heart clean, but when I start on one room, no sooner have I cleaned it than I discover another room is dirty. I begin on the second room, and the first one is already dusty again. I am not up to maintaining a clean heart and an obedient life!

Jesus reminded me, "You can't live out the Christian life in your own strength. That is impossible. Let me do it for you and through you. But I have no authority to take charge if the property is not mine."

In a flash it all became clear. Excitedly I exclaimed, "Lord, you have been my guest, and I have been trying to play the host. From now on you are going to be the owner and master of the house. I'm going to be the servant!"

Dropping to my knees, I presented the title deed to him: "Here it is, all that I am and have forever. Now you run the house. Just let me stay with you."

REFLECT: *Which is easier, being obedient to Christ while master of your own house, or being a servant of Christ in a home he tends to? How can you surrender more of yourself to him today?*

ROBERT BOYD MUNGER

Tackling Trials

> *Consider it pure joy, my brothers, whenever you face trials of many kinds,*
> *because you know that the testing of your faith develops perseverance.*

JAMES 1:2-3

James 1:2-3 is one of those passages that we like to quote to other people who are going through difficult times. But when we are in the storm we don't want to hear it. How is it possible to have joy in trials?

The key is in the word *consider*. It means "to think forward, to think about the outcome." People who have ambushed me with this verse usually get it wrong. They try to tell me to be happy about the pain. But pain is pain. The death of a friend still hurts. A business collapse still brings struggle. Joy comes when we realize what God will do in us as a result of the trial. We can have joy in our difficult days because we know we are going to come out on the other end more like Jesus.

REFLECT: *How have your experiences of trials strengthened your endurance and your ability to submit yourself to God?*

DOUGLAS CONNELLY

"If anyone would come after me,
he must deny himself and take up his cross and follow me."

MATTHEW 16:24

D r. Ben Carson, the brilliant African American surgeon, talks about his struggle with anger and the crucial decision he made that turned his life around. As a youth, he waged a fierce battle to control his temper. One day after a particularly nasty flare-up he decided to do something about his problem. Out of desperation he went into his small bathroom, closed the door and wrestled with God. After several hours, the young Carson emerged from that room a changed person.

Ben Carson went on to become a skilled surgeon and gained recognition for his part in the first successful separation of Siamese twins joined at the back of the head. Overcoming anger was a turning point in his life, and it did not happen by chance. It happened by choice.

Our deliverance from fear, anger, worry or doubt comes when we relinquish control of our lives to Christ. And this deliverance does not happen by chance. It happens by choice.

JOURNAL: *What emotions have the most power over you? How can you surrender those feelings to God?*

RAYMOND M. CAUSEY

Maundy Thursday

> For whenever you eat this bread and drink this cup,
> you proclaim the Lord's death until he comes.

1 CORINTHIANS 11:26

On the night before he died, Jesus gathered with his closest friends for the Passover meal. Startlingly, he washed their feet; somberly he taught them; and with a profound new meaning, he broke bread and poured wine. He intended that ever after, whenever his followers shared a meal, whenever they partook of the most common food and beverage, they would remember something, anticipate something and experience something.

At our meals we "give thanks," but do we remember that Jesus gave his body and blood for us? We "ask blessing," but do we anticipate the Great Feast Jesus will host in his kingdom? We "say grace," but do we experience the actual presence of Jesus? In our churches we celebrate the Lord's Supper or Eucharist or Mass as a solemn, even sacramental act, but Jesus doesn't require ceremony. He can open eyes to his presence at the table of any who remember him as they break bread together.

ACT: *How can you make more of your meals occasions to remember, anticipate and experience Jesus?*

BOBBY GROSS

F R I D A Y

Let us run with perseverance the race marked out for us.
Let us fix our eyes on Jesus, the author and perfecter of our faith,
who for the joy set before him endured the cross.

HEBREWS 12:1-2

For Jesus, the Friday of his crucifixion was torturous. So why do we call it "Good" Friday? Because, as Isaiah foretold, Christ was wounded for our sake. His bruises heal us; his punishment makes us whole. On Good Friday especially, we somberly meditate on the dark and glorious mystery of the cross.

Looking to Jesus, we gain strength to run our own race and endure our own sufferings, knowing that joy lies ahead, that we have the promise of healing and wholeness. Let it be so, not only this day but each time we slip a cross over our head or make its sign across our heart.

PRAY: *Oh Jesus, you pioneered my faith on the cross. Bring it one step closer to completion this day. Amen.*

BOBBY GROSS

> *Having been buried with him in baptism*
> *and raised with him through your faith in the power of God,*
> *who raised him from the dead.*

COLOSSIANS 2:12

In the early centuries of church history, baptism took place on Easter Sunday. How fitting! As Paul teaches, something profound happens to us in baptism: our repentant faith connects with God's transforming Spirit and, from that point on, we are united to Christ. His death becomes ours, and likewise his resurrection. With him we are "raised" to new life, and in him we are given a new self. The Spirit of power—who released Jesus from the tomb—steadily nurtures the new life and slowly shapes the new self. We do our part by continuing to discard old and unbecoming attitudes and behaviors and by continually putting on new clothes—Christlike ways of thinking and acting.

This season (and every other time) we celebrate Resurrection Day, so let's dress like it!

ACT: *What is one behavior you could take off this week? What is one you could put on?*

BOBBY GROSS

Spring

M O N D A Y

Making Your Heart a Home

"The Father . . . will give you another Counselor
to be with you forever—the Spirit of truth."

JOHN 14:16-17

My mother's mind, once sharp and active, is wasted by dementia. Her care-givers do not see the woman who sang in the church choir for sixty years and worked as a medical secretary for thirty years. They don't know the person who planted wildflowers, organized the historical pageant, wrote poetry and rescued every stray animal that came into the yard. It is up to me to explain, in disjointed fragments of information, who she is. The only people who truly know her are those who lived and worked with her before her illness.

Jesus promised his disciples that the Holy Spirit would live within them. Believers do not have to guess about who God is or what God is like. The Spirit of God has come to live in each of us. He knows us, and, even more remarkable, we can know him.

PRAY: *Thank God that he knows what is waiting for him as he makes his home in us.*

SANDY LARSEN

Auditor Only

> *Do not merely listen to the word, and so deceive yourselves.*
> *Do what it says.*

JAMES 1:22

A couple years ago I took a class at our local university. I paid my tuition and bought the books, but I registered as an auditor. I went to class, took notes and most of the time didn't have the foggiest idea what the professor was talking about. Anyone looking in on that class would have thought I was a real student, but on exam days I didn't show up. When semester projects were due, I didn't hand one in. When the grades came out, my report said, "No honor points, no academic credit, auditor only."

It's possible to go to church or a Bible study or to read a devotional book to hear God's Word and just be an auditor. What you hear doesn't really change your life. Auditors are never really involved in doing the assignments that God gives. Auditors never graduate.

ACT: *How can you enter fully into discipleship today?*

DOUGLAS CONNELLY

Get to Know the Guide

For this God is our God for ever and ever;
he will be our guide even to the end.

PSALM 48:14

Here are three clarifying thoughts about God's guidance: (1) God concerns himself more with our steps than with our overall journey; (2) God is more preoccupied with the present than with the future; and (3) God's will is that we purse the Guide more than guidance.

If the steps are more critical than the journey, and the present is of greater consequence than the future, and the Guide is more essential than the guidance, then we need to know the right step to take, we need to know what we must do in the present, and we need to know the Guide.

God does not guide us magically; he guides us relationally. Divine guidance grows out of a conversational relationship with our heavenly Father. We may seek guidance, but God provides something better: himself.

REFLECT: *Are you more preoccupied with the present or the future? How can your relationship with God be more grounded in his presence than his guidance?*

RICK EZELL

THURSDAY

I Have Everything I Need

The LORD is my shepherd, I shall not be in want.

PSALM 23:1

I love the simple words that open the Twenty-Third Psalm. We don't like to look at need because we see it as weakness, maybe even sin. But, as Mother Teresa expressed, "the fullness of our hearts is expressed in . . . the way we need." When I lay my need on the table, I see what I need release from: sin, loss, worry, fear, loneliness, confusion—the list is long.

Julian of Norwich expresses well the place of need in our hearts: "You are enough for me and I can ask for nothing . . . less which can pay you full worship. And if I ask for anything . . . less, always I am in want, but only in you do I have everything."

There is only one response to my need. Jesus has everything I need because he is everything I need.

JOURNAL: *Present your heart's need to God and ask him to be everything that you need.*

MARSHA CROCKETT

F R I D A Y   *The Bridegroom Is Here*

"How can the guests of the bridegroom fast while he is with them?"

MARK 2:19

One afternoon a group of college students were studying Mark 2 in the school's library. It was close to the time for midterm exams, and many of the students were anxious about the amount of work still ahead of them. One student spoke up: "It seems as long as Jesus is with us, we must celebrate."

The group sat quietly—this was not what they had expected to hear. But the more they looked, the more deeply they understood: Jesus' people are to mourn at the appropriate time but commanded to live in the presence of the bridegroom.

That night at midnight (a peak study hour), the students simultaneously threw open their dorm windows and yelled, "The bridegroom is here!" Then they returned to studying, knowing they were in the presence of God.

R E F L E C T : *How can you choose to celebrate Jesus' presence in the face of anxiety or under pressure?*

ALISON SIEWERT

Rebuilt—Not Remodeled

*For we are God's workmanship, created in Christ Jesus to do good works,
which God prepared in advance for us to do.*

EPHESIANS 2:10

Jesus' goal is never to remodel but to rebuild. He wants us to be glorious, not so-so. God's gracious acceptance of us is a gift, received through faith, pure and simple. But once received, his grace continues to work in us as holy love, empowering us to become what he made us to be from the beginning: his "workmanship, created in Christ Jesus to do good works, which God prepared in advance for us to do." The requirement remains, but with it comes the means to meet it. Augustine understood this grace when he prayed, "Give what you command, and command whatever you want."

PRAY: *Pray Augustine's prayer today, calling to mind some of God's commands as you do.*

BEN PATTERSON

MONDAY

The Study

> *Jesus did many other things as well.*
> *If every one of them were written down,*
> *I suppose that even the whole world would not have room*
> *for the books that would be written.*

JOHN 21:25

My favorite scene in Disney's *Beauty and the Beast* is the one where Belle enters the castle library and sees books in every direction, from floor to ceiling. My house is not quite that well stocked, but within its walls are sixteen bookcases containing several thousand books. Categorized and alphabetized, they range across the various genres of fiction and literature, history and social issues, biography and memoir, spirituality and theology.

But quite often my book collection outgrows the available space and begins to get a little cluttered. Books accumulate on the dining room table, on the kitchen counter, on top of the washer and dryer.

My mind can likewise be far too cluttered with distractions that are taking me in too many different directions. I suspect that Jesus would encourage me to get a grip, weed out some unnecessary volumes and prioritize my reading list.

ACT: *Besides the Bible, what books have helped shape your spiritual life? Find a spiritual classic and read through it.*

AL HSU

Flitting Thoughts

> *When our fathers were in Egypt, they gave no thought to your miracles;*
> *they did not remember your many kindnesses.*

PSALM 106:7

The bird feeder outside our office window is both a delight and a distraction. Today the feeder has constant traffic. Mostly it's cardinals, titmice, woodpeckers, nuthatches and chickadees. But a few minutes ago, when I should have been busy searching for Scripture, I jumped up and rushed to the window. A warbler! What kind? Where's the bird book? Warblers . . . without wing bars . . . Hold still, bird; stop flitting!

I suppose we should know better than to have a feeder outside our office window, but the feeder was there first, before the room became an office, and the birds were already accustomed to it. So goes our reasoning.

The thoughts that distract us from God's purposes are not always ugly. They may be as attractive as the sudden appearance of a warbler, but they are still distractions. We need the Spirit's discipline to keep our minds focused on God.

REFLECT: *What distracts you from your focus on Christ? Become more aware of those distractions and let God recapture your thoughts.*

SANDY LARSEN

Whatever Is Pure

Whatever is true, whatever is noble, whatever is right,
whatever is pure . . . think about such things.

PHILIPPIANS 4:8

I love great fiction. But one winter, I buried myself in dime-store romances, plowing through one book after another. Vaguely, I sensed my escapism, but I set aside that discomfiture and kept reading. While I curled up on the sofa, lethargic, my family life disintegrated. I couldn't pay attention to the children. I didn't want to be with my husband. Scripture was the last thing on my mind. I certainly didn't want to think about what these avoidances said about my heart and my relationships with family, friends and God.

Finally, winter thaws inched us toward Easter. The junk welled up within me so thickly that I stashed the stack of books in the resale bag, refusing to indulge in anything except Scripture or contemplative reading until we celebrated the resurrection. Slowly, my hard heart softened and God began wooing me with his Word. I could move toward my family again with a pure heart. Fasting from unrealistic fiction broke the chains and set me free to really live once again.

JOURNAL: *What are some ways you're tempted to escape? What can you do to help ground yourself in reality?*

JANE RUBIETTA

Ever~Deepening Thoughts

My soul finds rest in God alone.

PSALM 62:1

I can be restless, my mind astir with minor problems, tasks to accomplish and unmet expectations. I can feel desperate, seeking more of something—more calmness, more quiet, more open space and available time. My life is sometimes mired in hectic, harried schemes, my world at times shackled in wars and rumors of wars. I sometimes feel cemented in by asphalt and cars, buildings and fences.

When I look to the Source of life, he brings me to a place of peace. Only in God does my soul rest, touching his beauty in ever-deepening thoughts and sighs, voices and silences. He turns the stirred-up surface of my life into his beautiful dwelling place.

REFLECT: *What keeps your mind weary? Close your eyes and picture the cross at a distance. Slowly make your way toward it until you can kneel at the foot of the crucified Jesus and rest in the shadow of grace.*

MARSHA CROCKETT

F R I D A Y *Discipleship of the Mind*

We take captive every thought to make it obedient to Christ.

2 CORINTHIANS 10:5

Anti-intellectualism has a long and sordid history in American evangelicalism. This sentiment was perhaps best captured by the evangelist Billy Sunday: "If I had a million dollars, I'd give $999,999 to the church and $1 to education." Yet our ability to think is one of God's greatest gifts to us. To be created in his image means to be able to reason, create and synthesize. As Abraham Kuyper noted, "There is not a square inch of the entire creation about which Jesus Christ does not cry, 'This is mine! This belongs to me!'" As such, every aspect of our life—including our intellect—rightly belongs to him. Our calling includes discipling our mind and actively engaging in the marketplace of ideas.

JOURNAL: *List the ways you bring your mind under the lordship of Jesus. What activities do you need to add?*

ALEC HILL

Change the Way You Think

For as he thinks within himself, so he is.

PROVERBS 23:7 NASB

At one time in my life, my thoughts chronically edged toward resentment as I rehashed an old family wound. My mental ward filled with arguments; they spilled out in my home, contaminating my relationships with their ugly breath.

My thought life needed help. I had to start by acknowledging my pain, my woundedness. Making God privy to the pain dulled its edge, initiating healing. Then, when anger bristled, I recognized it as pain's signal, moved back to God and started taking the others who were involved in the situation to him as well. My heart began to break for them, for the pain that had jump-started their anger.

Healing our thoughts is a long process; it took months for me to move from anger to compassion, to change the default pattern of my thoughts. My mental ward is much nicer these days, but the conscious choice remains daily: change the way I think, change the way I feel and act.

REFLECT: *Pick one sin pattern in your thought life. Bring it to God and see what he does.*

JANE RUBIETTA

M O N D A Y *The Dining Room*

> *"Why spend money on what is not bread,*
> *and your labor on what does not satisfy?*
> *Listen, listen to me, and eat what is good,*
> *and your soul will delight in the richest of fare."*

ISAIAH 55:2

I've often thought that if there is a Madison Avenue theory of human nature it is best expressed by Sesame Street's Cookie Monster: See cookie, want cookie, eat cookie. Some of the brightest minds in the world stay up late at night looking for ways to convince us that we are nothing more than a collection of appetites that must be gratified. The writers of Scripture, though, were convinced that the mere indulging of appetite is not the fulfillment of human nature, only the sure destruction of it. Our appetites are good things, but they must be tamed. They are, to paraphrase Dallas Willard, good servants but poor masters. Desire serves us well when it hungers for that which matters most.

PRAY: *What do you hunger for? Ask God to keep your appetite in line with his will.*

JOHN ORTBERG

Not-So-Bad Sins

I warn you, as I did before,
that those who live like this will not inherit the kingdom of God.

GALATIANS 5:21

I wanted to memorize Galatians 5:16-26 because it discusses the battle between our sinful nature and the Spirit. It goes on to tell of the beautiful fruit of the Spirit. But when I read verses 19-20 I thought, *Yuck! I'm going to skip that part!*

Sexual immorality, debauchery, hatred, idolatry, witchcraft, drunkenness, orgies . . . Without a doubt they are acts of a sinful nature. God has every right to soundly condemn anyone who would engage in such awful things. But they had nothing to do with me.

On closer reading, however, some words caught my eye and made me squirm: *jealousy, envy, selfish ambition.* Uh oh. How could it be that those "not-so-bad" sins—ones I saw in myself—were mixed right in among the awful sins I felt were so far beneath me?

I realized that God made no distinction between the "not-so-bad" and the "horrible." I went back and memorized the entire passage.

REFLECT: *Read through the list of sins in Galatians 5:19-21. Are there things you need to commit to the Lord in prayer?*

KAY MARSHALL STROM

WEDNESDAY

David pleaded with God for the child. He fasted and went into his house.

2 SAMUEL 12:16

My stomach growls, reminding me of my promise to fast and pray on behalf of a family member who is having a persistent problem. It doesn't seem a big thing to go without food for a short time, and liquids stave off any headache that might come about from abstaining, but how hard it is to wean myself from food's instant satisfaction and the habit of eating whenever I want.

Prayer during each rumbling not only helps me stick it out, it also changes my heart in the process. I find myself calmer, more present, more thoughtful. Even better, my attitude moves from judgment to grace, from hurt to compassion, from numbness to tears, from fear to anticipation. When I bow my head for a moment, it feels as though I am entering into a huge, spacious place, like eternity. That is just where God longs to bring the loved one I pray for—and me as well.

REFLECT: *Where might God be leading you regarding fasting? What fears do you feel when you think of the possibilities?*

JANE RUBIETTA

Laughter at Dinner

> *Our mouths were filled with laughter,*
> *our tongues with songs of joy.*
>
> PSALM 126:2

Not long ago I invited some friends to dinner who were struggling in their marriage. Worried about the tension we might all feel, I prayed that Christ would minister in just the right way during our time together. Although I was able to listen to them as they voiced some of their struggles, the real ministry occurred at the dinner table when a silly remark sent them both into fits of laughter. "It's been a long time since we've laughed like that. But it was exactly what we needed," they said. While the laughter hasn't cured their problem, it opened up a window of refreshment where they could breathe in the fresh air of hope.

JOURNAL: *What part does laughter play in your daily life? What part has laughter played in the care of your soul?*

MARSHA CROCKETT

FRIDAY

The Stranglehold of Stuff

*"Seek first his kingdom and his righteousness,
and all these things will be given to you as well."*

MATTHEW 6:33

Albert Schweitzer was a medical missionary who died in 1965 at the age of ninety. His standard attire was a white pith helmet, a white shirt, pants and a black tie. He had worn one hat for forty years, the tie for twenty. Told one day that some men owned dozens of neckties, Schweitzer remarked, "For one neck?"

When we place our relationship with Christ first in our heart, we will gain a new perspective. The things that from our vantage point seemed necessary will no longer be important. When we state a magnificent "yes" to God's rule in our life, we will have the courage to say "no" to secondary pursuits. When we seek God's reign and rule in our life first, everything necessary will fall in its proper order. Everything hinges upon keeping first things first.

JOURNAL: *Take stock of your life. Where does the accumulation of things rank in relation to your relationship with Christ?*

RICK EZELL

Come to the Table

"If anyone hears my voice and opens the door,
I will . . . eat with him, and he with me."

R E V E L A T I O N   3 : 2 0

When I first read Revelation 3:20, I thought of fellowship with Jesus as a meal he served, where I only had to show up at the table and eat what was offered. I could then walk away warmed and filled. But I have since learned that times of fellowship are for both of us. I am eating a shared meal, not a solitary one, and if I don't show up for that meal, Jesus goes away hungry. There are words he longs to say to me. They are my food and drink. There are also words he longs to hear from me. My words of love are his daily bread.

Realizing that, I suddenly felt guilty for all the times he had hungered for my fellowship and I hadn't been there to give it. But then I looked into his eyes, and I realized something else: He doesn't want me to feel guilty. He wants me to feel in love.

P R A Y : *Approach Jesus today with the assurance that he longs to have your company.*

KEN GIRE

MONDAY *The Living Room*

"Whoever comes to me I will never drive away."

JOHN 6:37

My living room is a quiet, comfortable room with a warm atmosphere. Jesus saw it and promised, "I will be here every morning early. Meet me here and we will start the day together."

So, morning after morning, I would go downstairs to the living room. Through the Bible and his Holy Spirit he would talk to me. In prayer I would respond. Our friendship deepened in these quiet times of personal conversation.

However, under the pressure of many responsibilities, little by little, this time began to be shortened. Eventually I began to miss days now and then. One morning, I recall rushing down the steps in a hurry to be on my way to an important appointment.

As I passed the living room, the door was open. Glancing in I saw a fire in the fireplace and Jesus sitting there. I stopped, turned and hesitantly went in. "Master, I'm sorry! Have you been here every morning?"

"Yes," he said. "I told you I would be here to meet with you. Don't neglect this hour, if only for my sake. Whether or not you want to be with me, remember I want to be with you. I really love you!"

REFLECT: *What people and things distract you from "quiet times of personal conversation"? How can you better protect your time with Christ?*

ROBERT BOYD MUNGER

The Good Guest

> *"Martha, Martha . . . you are worried and upset about many things,*
> *but only one thing is needed."*
>
> LUKE 10:41-42

I love my kitchen. It's an abundant place where I work hard to prepare good stuff for my family and friends. The kitchen is where we meet Martha too, working away, making sure the snacks are in order for Jesus' visit. Pots clang and flour flies as she anxiously plays host. And that is precisely the problem: she plays host, but Jesus is looking for guests. It's his party; he is always the host, and we are always the guests. We only think we are hosting, and our pride confronts us when we learn that all Jesus wants is for us to hang out with him. There is nothing we can add to him, no party we can throw. The house is not ours but his. He throws the party; we come, invited not to provide but to be provided for.

REFLECT: *How have you been caught up in thinking that you needed to do things for God? Consider how you might become a guest.*

ALISON SIEWERT

Perfect in His Sight

He has made perfect forever those who are being made holy.

HEBREWS 10:14

All our sins—past, present and future—are forgiven the moment we receive Christ. You may ask, "Why do I need to confess my sins?" Confession is an act of obedience and an expression of faith, making real in our experience what is true from God's point of view. Through Christ's sacrifice, God sees us as righteous and perfect, but daily we are becoming in our experience what we already are in his sight.

This maturing process is accelerated through studying God's Word, prayer, witnessing and "spiritual breathing." When you retake control of your life, you need to breathe spiritually. First, exhale by confession. "If we confess our sins, he is faithful and just and will forgive us our sins and purify us from all unrighteousness" (1 John 1:9). Next, inhale by appropriating the fullness of God's Spirit by faith.

PRAY: *Today practice confession and the refreshment of breathing out sin and breathing in the fullness of the Spirit (Ephesians 5:18).*

BILL BRIGHT

A Room Full of Quiet

Much dreaming and many words are meaningless.
Therefore stand in awe of God.

ECCLESIASTES 5:7

Recently I accompanied a teenaged boy to court. As his family and I entered the courtroom, we saw several dozen other people waiting for their turn in the courtroom. Yet, despite the number of people around, it was deathly still in the courthouse.

I have noticed the same silence in the waiting rooms of doctors' and dentists' offices. It is a breath-holding kind of quiet, the stillness of people who are about to place themselves in the hands of authority and cannot guarantee the outcome. Their mouths are shut by the presence of something bigger than themselves.

I appreciate our church's radio ministry, but sometimes I regret it too. Radio cannot tolerate dead air time. Something audible must always be going on. In the urge for "many words," do we neglect to "stand in awe of God"? At times silence is our best response to God. When we are quiet, we give him a chance to speak to us.

REFLECT: *Do you talk too much to or about God and neglect to listen? Take some time to listen today.*

SANDY LARSEN

F R I D A Y
What a Friend We Have in Jesus

"I no longer call you servants. . . . Instead, I have called you friends,
for everything that I learned from my Father I have made known to you."

J O H N   1 5 : 1 5

Recently, when I read John 15:15, I got a picture in my mind of a cupped hand framing the corner of a mouth, lips nearly brushing another's ear and whispered words bringing delight to the hearer's ears. The picture was of intimate friendship, which is what Jesus offers in this passage.

Jesus reveals to us those secret mysteries passed to him by his Father. He doesn't keep them to himself; he shares the joy. Jesus, in his great love and generosity, gives all that he has to the ones he calls "friends."

I'm good at being friends with a lot of people. But I realized I've not been so good at being friends with Jesus. I can sometimes find myself going through an entire day not thinking about him once. And yet, this picture of the cupped hand awakens in me the realization that Jesus is always near, always speaking, always pursuing.

PRAY: *Jesus, give me ears to hear. Remind me of your presence throughout the day.*

CAROLYN CARNEY

A River of Life

> *"The water I give him will become in him a spring of water*
> *welling up to eternal life."*

JOHN 4:14

Rich left for his night job with an argument still lingering in the air. Our tiny efficiency apartment closed in around me as I felt the aftermath of my ugly behavior and the scarring on our relationship. I puttered around, feeling worse by the minute. Finally, I got on my knees and begged God to forgive me, to rectify the problem I'd created in our young marriage.

God moved me on in prayer for my husband, who was loading freight trucks in the stultifying summer night. The words to a song we sang with our youth group came to mind: "I've got a river of life, flowing out of me . . ."

The next morning, Rich smiled at me and said, "Last night was so hot. I was drenched, and then this song came to me . . ." I was shushed by new awareness of the power of forgiveness and the presence of the Holy Spirit.

ACT: *Follow any impulses to pray for people in your life, to confess your sins against them, to seek reconciliation with them.*

JANE RUBIETTA

MONDAY

The Workroom

"Apart from me you can do nothing."

JOHN 15:5

Jesus entered my workroom and looked over the talents and skills I had. He said, "This is fairly well furnished. What are you producing with your life for the kingdom of God?"

I told him, "I'm ashamed to say that with my awkwardness and limited ability, I don't think I'll ever do much."

Putting his great strong arms around me and his hands under mine, Jesus picked up the tools and began to work through me. "Relax. You are still too tense. Let go—let me do the work!"

It amazes me what his skilled hands can do through mine if I only trust him and let him have his way. I am very far from satisfied with the product that is being turned out. I still get in his way at times. There's much more that I need to learn. But I do know that whatever has been produced for God has been through him and through the power of his Spirit in me.

REFLECT: *What skills and talents can you give to Christ? He will surprise you with what he can do through you!*

ROBERT BOYD MUNGER

Searching for Socks

I love the house where you live, O LORD,
the place where your glory dwells.

PSALM 26:8

Today I washed sixteen socks. None of them matched. So I went on a rampage until I paired fourteen of them, and the two that were left earned a place in the garbage. While nations negotiate peace or wage war, while relief organizations combat world hunger, while scientists explore the universe, I contemplate lost socks. And what impact does my dedication to the Lost Sock Society make? Fewer sweaty feet, fewer blisters? What a reward.

There are some things in life that we just have to deal with, and they may not carry any spiritual depth beyond what meets the eye. Here's the simple truth I found while hunting socks: If I want to wear socks, I have to keep track of them. But menial chores don't have to be meaningless, for it is in such places where Christ meets me, where he comes to walk beside me as a friend through my ordinary routines.

JOURNAL: *How can Jesus' companionship affect how you go about the most mundane tasks of your daily work?*

MARSHA CROCKETT

Heavenly Minded

Set your minds on things above, not on earthly things.

COLOSSIANS 3:2

Some people get the wrong impression when the Bible talks about being heavenly minded. They think obeying Paul's command will get them in trouble. Suppertime will roll around and nothing will be prepared because they have been praying all day. The boss will get angry because they're reading the Bible at work instead of doing what they're paid to do.

But Paul doesn't mean that when our minds are set on heavenly things we will lose interest in our responsibilities on earth. What Paul means is this: when we set our minds on Christ, it completely changes our attitude toward things on earth. We prepare a meal for our families with God's glory in mind. We study for an algebra test not to impress a teacher but to please Christ. We do our jobs as if Jesus is our boss. We still carry out all the responsibilities of life but for a new reason. We do it all, even the most menial task, for Christ's approval.

ACT: *Pick one task from your schedule today and determine to do it in such a way that Christ is pleased.*

DOUGLAS CONNELLY

Finish What You Start

*Now finish the work, so that your eager willingness to do it
may be matched by your completion of it.*

2 CORINTHIANS 8:11

A real estate agent once showed us through a house that was a museum of unfinished projects. Someone had started to paint a room and quit in mid-brushstroke. In another room, half of a wall was paneled; in still another room the paint was stripped off half of the woodwork. We didn't buy the house, but whoever did continued the legacy of unfinished projects. The old siding was removed and the house was wrapped in new silvery insulation—and it stayed that way for a year!

It is easy to jump into the adventure of a pioneering ministry or some new task that we feel God wants us to do. But before we jump, we should search our hearts to be sure we mean to continue. Do we intend to see the job through to completion? It is better to start something small and finish it than to start something big and leave it half done.

PRAY: *Pray for the means and the courage to finish what you start and the wisdom not to start what you can't finish.*

SANDY LARSEN

F R I D A Y

"I will give you a new heart and put a new spirit in you;
I will remove from you your heart of stone and give you a heart of flesh . . .
and move you to follow my decrees."

EZEKIEL 36:26-27

Though thousands of immigrants came through Ellis Island in the nineteenth and early twentieth centuries, some were turned back soon after they arrived. Immigrants would climb several flights of stairs to an examination area. Those who struggled would be pulled out of the crowd and sent back to the boats.

God can sometimes seem like a doctor scrutinizing us from the top of the stairs. Who can possibly be holy as he is holy? But imagine a doctor running down the stairs to someone who is struggling. He helps her to the examination area, where he administers food and antibiotics. Then he checks her into a hospital, personally covering all her expenses. When she is released, the doctor takes her into his home.

That would be like God. God calls us to a high calling but carries us there and back home with him.

PRAY: *Ask God to give you what you need to achieve his high calling today.*

BEN PATTERSON

Two are better than one,
because they have a good return for their work.

ECCLESIASTES 4:9

The Batcave may well be the coolest place ever conceived. It's command central in the war against crime; it lies deep in the belly of the earth, far from silly entertainments that might distract its occupants from their mission; and it's stocked to the stalactites with advanced technology and weaponry—what one star-eyed observer referred to as "wonderful toys."

Batman built the Batcave to taste. It's efficient and pragmatic, but it's also cold and dreary. Other heroes may respect what Batman has accomplished in his cave, but nobody really wants to join him there.

We're taught to stay on task, and that's generally a good thing, but the better we get at it, the more distant our lives get from the people we work with, the people we live with. From the beginning God commanded us to work because he didn't want us to be idle, but in the beginning he made more than one of us because he didn't want us to be alone.

REFLECT: *How can you make connections with other people without neglecting your responsibilities today?*

DAVID A. ZIMMERMAN

MONDAY *The Recreation Room*

Rejoice in the Lord always. I will say it again: Rejoice!

PHILIPPIANS 4:4

As a baseball game progresses, a team may be down by several runs, but until the final out is called, there is still a chance, still hope. Many games are won in the final inning.

Often, believers look like a team that is down by several runs with two outs in the last inning. The good news is that we already know the outcome of the game. We win. *We win!*

As creatures made in God's image, we are to reflect his fierce joy in life. This joy is the outward expression of the inward knowledge that God has everything under control. It is the knowledge that the game is not over, that in the end, because of Christ, we win. This infectious joy convinces a watching world that Christ can transform a life—no matter what the circumstances. Let us express the "joy, joy, joy, joy down in our hearts."

ACT: *Go ahead and laugh a lot today. You know you want to.*

RICK EZELL

Chain of Events

"I know the plans I have for you . . .
plans to prosper you and not to harm you,
plans to give you hope and a future."

JEREMIAH 29:11

Funny how one casual "yes" can set an entire chain of events into motion and move us unwittingly into the stream of God's plans. My buddy Joe asked me to audition for summer theater after my sophomore year in college; we both got parts, and Angela, the female lead, became my friend and Joe's girlfriend. Back on campus, who should sit behind me in Finite Math but Angela? We rented a house together for the rest of college, and the Christmas of my senior year I dragged her to a regional conference for a campus Christian group. At the conference on the final day, on the up escalator at a Chicago hotel, I met the man I would eventually marry. Twenty-three years later, we're still going up, and I owe it all to Rodgers and Hammerstein—and God, who takes an interest in the tiniest circumstances of our lives, delighting when we say yes.

REFLECT: *Which of your "yeses" opened up a new world of life, of ministry, of hope?*

JANE RUBIETTA

The Art of Contemplation

"See, the LORD has chosen Bezalel . . .
and he has filled him with the Spirit of God, with skill,
ability and knowledge in all kinds of crafts—to make artistic designs."

EXODUS 35:30-32

We tend to think being filled with the Holy Spirit is for "spiritual" purposes such as preaching or healing or worship. It may be surprising, then, to read of Bazalel, the Spirit-filled artist who was gifted for creating and crafting. Maybe our notion of what is spiritual needs to expand.

Each year I take my son to the Metropolitan Museum of Art to look at works that depict the Passion. We allow artists to help us apprehend the truth and grace of Jesus. And a few years ago, I bought my first painting. It was a startling image of a lovely pair of feathered wings attached to a bird-like skeleton that was gliding over a black deep. It became for me a metaphor for the reanimation of something fallen, grace overcoming the gravity of sin. In short, the painting preached to me. Contemplating it brought healing and moved me to deeper worship.

ACT: *What visual creations help you contemplate the things of God? Schedule some time to spend with such creations.*

BOBBY GROSS

Let us fix our eyes on Jesus, the author and perfecter of our faith.

HEBREWS 12:2

For me, middle school gym class was always a welcome break from the normal school routine—except on those days when we were herded into the gym along with the girls' class for instruction in ballroom dancing. In seventh grade, the last thing I wanted to do was stand close to a girl. Ballroom dancing days were an exercise in fear and intimidation. And all the while, the girls kept telling us how graceful this was, how wonderful, how romantic. I remember thinking, "I wish this girl would just leave me alone and let me try to get these stupid steps right."

But of course, that was precisely the point we missed: ballroom dancing is not just about getting the steps right; it's about a growing relationship with your partner. It's about moving together in an embrace of openness and developing a growing intimacy with your partner.

Have you made the same mistake, approaching the Christian life as if it were about getting the steps right? Begin with fellowship and watch it mature into fruitfulness (see John 15:4-9).

REFLECT: *Do you tend more toward rules or more toward relationship? How could your current relationships better support your desire to grow in Christlikeness?*

DUFFY ROBBINS

Clean Up Your Room

"Sell your possessions, and give alms.
Make purses for yourselves that do not wear out,
an unfailing treasure in heaven."

LUKE 12:33-34 NRSV

Like most parents, I periodically sigh at the doors of my kids' disheveled rooms. I wish they'd pick up after themselves, but I know that's about as likely to occur as, say, armadillos developing wings.

When we started packing to move, I realized why my kids had struggled to keep their rooms from complete disaster: they have too much stuff. From birthday presents to hand-me-down clothes to cherished carnival prizes, their rooms are too full because they have too many things to fill them.

My life is no different. I look around my office and see too much stuff. Western culture's romance with the material has produced unmentionable quantities of plastics, tiny toy parts and paper packaging. We have managed to overwhelm ourselves with unhealthy stuff in decadent quantities.

To us, Jesus offers some challenging advice: "Sell your possessions, and give money away." As tough as getting an armadillo to grow wings? Perhaps, but with God all things are possible.

PRAY: *Ask Jesus for help to keep your house from becoming overcrowded.*

ALISON SIEWERT

Don't Just Stand There

*"Why do you stand here looking into the sky?
This same Jesus, who has been taken from you into heaven,
will come back in the same way you have seen him go into heaven."*

ACTS 1:11

We are rightly awed by the fact of Jesus' rising to "the right hand of the Father" and rightly fascinated by the promise of his return in fierce glory. But sometimes we overdo it. We focus on the otherworldly and obsess about the second coming, and the men in white who spoke these words gently rebuke us.

Don't stand staring; get busy! We watch for him, yes, but our watching is in our worship, in our witness, in our work. We pray daily to our enthroned Leader, "Let your kingdom come. Let it come as I do my job; let it come as I befriend my neighbor; let it come as I say my prayers. Risen and returning Lord, let it come."

REFLECT: *In remembrance of Ascension Day (traditionally the first Sunday in May), reflect on the Ascension as a starting point for your ministry.*

BOBBY GROSS

MONDAY

The Bedroom

> *How lovely is your dwelling place, O LORD Almighty!*
>
> PSALM 84:1

Returning home from a weekend away, I'm in bed early, anxious to nestle down into the comfort of my own bed, my own surroundings, simple and worn as they are. I thank God for the familiar comfort of my own blankets and the sounds of the squeaky springs in my mattress. "Getting away" seems a distant desire when coming home renews sweet contentment and a realization that this place of rest is where I belong.

So too is the sense of comfort when we return to the Father after feeling far away. Like the prodigal running into his Father's arms, the desire to get away evaporates in the embrace of faithful love, like a bed always ready to be occupied by the one who belongs there. But this place of rest is also available to the one who remains faithful to the Father in season and out. For he renews the heart with sweet contentment day by day when I nestle down into his mercy and compassion, knowing this is where I belong.

PRAY: *Confess any ways you feel distant from God today. Run to him with your desire to abide in him more closely.*

MARSHA CROCKETT

Indoor Voice

He grants sleep to those he loves.

PSALM 127:2

It was our first time baby-sitting our niece Olivia. I got to read a bedtime story with my wife at my side and my niece in my lap. Olivia chose *Goodnight Moon*.

I began with great enthusiasm. "GOODNIGHT, ROOM!" My niece giggled and kicked as I extroverted its words with reckless abandon.

My wife, however, gave me a nudge that reminded me of our mission. We were getting our niece ready to sleep, not to party all night. I adjusted my voice from its "outdoor" setting to a more appropriate level: "Goodnight, moon . . ."

Like me, two-year-olds have little interest in going to sleep. But no matter how hard we fight it, rest is an inevitability, and it deserves to be embraced. God in his sovereignty ordains rest for us so we may be restored for our next adventure.

In the end, God's rest will initiate us into an eternal celebration. Until then, sleep is a reminder that we are watched over by One who keeps our souls through the night and again through the day.

PRAY: *Tonight, when you lay down to sleep, pray the Lord your soul to keep.*

DAVID A. ZIMMERMAN

Big Boys and Bad Dreams

The LORD is good to all; He has compassion on all he has made.
The LORD is near to all who call on him.

PSALM 145:9, 18

Sometimes my son, Spencer, wakes up from his nap feeling happy, and he lies in bed for awhile humming to himself. Eventually, he might call me or venture downstairs on his own. Today, however, Spencer woke up from his nap crying and calling, "Mommy!"

I went into his room and hugged him. Then I asked why he was crying. He said, "Sometimes big boys have bad dreams." He sucked on his pacifier reflectively, then added, "And sometimes big boys call their mommies."

I guess at three Spencer is already experiencing some external pressure to let go of Mommy. Our culture is teaching him the virtues of independence and autonomy. But these are not Christian virtues. Christianity teaches us dependence.

We never outgrow our need to call on God. As a matter of fact, learning this God-dependence is the surest path to maturity. The bigger we get, the more we need God.

JOURNAL: *Recall with thankfulness a time that you have called and God has come to you.*

CINDY BUNCH

Holy Kisses

Above all else, guard your heart.

PROVERBS 4:23

The first one ever to kiss us was our heavenly Father when he breathed his life into each of us. It has always been God's hope that those made most like him will one day return those kisses.

This subject of holy kisses can be difficult for some of us. We might have grown up not feeling truly worthy of unconditional kisses. Or maybe we believe that no one kisses us without wanting something in return. Though the intimate contact might be enjoyable, our souls know that such a kiss is taking rather than giving, a feigned expression of affection to possess or control, not to bless and endow. Only the Father's kisses can always be an exhalation of blessing, an unconditional gift of life and love.

REFLECT: *Spend some time enjoying the intimacy God offers at no cost.*

KEN FONG

Our Husband

> *"For your Maker is your husband—the LORD Almighty is his name."*
>
> ISAIAH 54:5

Recently I was told the apartment I rent would be sold. I hate moving. I especially hate being forced to move. And doing it alone, as a single woman, makes me feel all the more vulnerable. It is these times when I miss the protection of a husband.

For a single-income missionary to find a reasonably priced urban apartment is rather like finding that proverbial needle in the haystack. I grew anxious. I sent an e-mail to friends requesting prayer and fell into bed. After tossing and turning for a while, I finally remembered Isaiah 54:5. I prayed, "God, I need you to be my husband in this. I need your protection." Then I drifted off to sleep.

The next morning, I received a reply from a friend: "I've been praying to your HUSBAND about this today and He assured me He'd take care of it." Indeed he did.

Being single in a coupled world has not been easy. But it becomes more manageable when I choose to live as though I belong to God.

REFLECT: *In what way do you need God to provide for you today?*

CAROLYN CARNEY

"Peace be with you! As the Father has sent me, I am sending you."
And with that he breathed on them and said, "Receive the Holy Spirit."

JOHN 20:21-22

On Pentecost Sunday, the church worldwide marks the outpouring of the Holy Spirit on ten dozen disciples that occurred some fifteen days after Jesus' death. Acts 2 depicts the dramatic episode, complete with tornadolike roaring, floating flames and exclamations in languages never learned. What power!

But power for what? John records an earlier, more intimate impartation of the Spirit. Jesus had inexplicably appeared—alive!—among his hiding followers and had given them a profound commission: "I'm sending you as I was sent" (see John 20:21). They were to be little Jesuses, not divine in themselves but inhabited by the Divine. Then Jesus breathed on them, a physical portrayal of the spiritual gift.

We too are "sent ones." Our mission? Like Jesus, we are to announce and embody the kingdom of God in the world. Our means? Like Jesus, we can do God's work only by the empowering presence of the Spirit.

PRAY: *Ask God to refresh you with his powerful Spirit and to show you again what he has sent you to do.*

BOBBY GROSS

MONDAY *The Hall Closet*

You restored me to health and let me live.

ISAIAH 38:16

I had given Jesus access to all the rooms of my heart. But in my closet, behind lock and key, were dead and rotting things left over from the old life—not wicked, but not right and good to have in a Christian life. Yet I wanted them so much for myself I was afraid to admit they were there. I did not want Christ to see them.

Jesus brought me to the closet and pointed at the door. "There's a peculiar odor in there! Some dead thing! I will take my bed out on the back porch or somewhere else. I'm certainly not going to stay around that."

When you have come to know and love Jesus Christ, one of the worst things that can happen is to sense him withdrawing his face. "I'll give you the key," I said sadly, "but you'll have to clean it out. I haven't the strength to do it."

What a release and victory to have those dead things out of my life! Immediately a fresh, fragrant breeze swept through the house. The whole atmosphere of my heart changed when Jesus cleaned and restored it.

REFLECT: *What memories would you like to see healed and made whole by Jesus? What stands in the way of his doing his work?*

ROBERT BOYD MUNGER

Tattoos and All

> *But God demonstrates his own love for us in this:*
> *While we still were sinners, Christ died for us.*

ROMANS 5:8

In the movie *Dead Man Walking*, Poncelet, a young convict on death row, is befriended by a nun. A depth of relationship is reached when Poncelet finally admits his ugly crime to himself and to her.

My favorite scene is the one in which the nun finds Poncelet in his undershirt, exposing all of his tattoos. He's embarrassed and believes that she will think badly of him. All along he's been hiding the really awful stuff on the inside, and now he's afraid to expose his tattoos. But the nun had realized that Poncelet was hiding more than tattoos long before that moment, and she chose to love him anyway.

This is the greatest gift an intimate relationship can offer—to know that we have been accepted and forgiven in the full knowledge of who we are, complete with sin, scars and tattoos. This is what Jesus offers us. There is no need to hide. Just let the grace pour over you.

REFLECT: *Allow yourself to sit for a time in God's lavish grace.*

CAROLYN CARNEY

WEDNESDAY

Let us then approach the throne of grace with confidence,
so that we may receive mercy and find grace to help us in our time of need.

HEBREWS 4:16

How can we approach the throne of grace boldly when we feel like the scum of the earth? We can only do it by admitting that we are broken and acknowledging that God's grace is bigger than our sin. Jesus, before breathing his last on the cross, pleaded, "Father, forgive them, for they do not know what they are doing" (Luke 23:34). He understands our brokenness.

Eugene O'Neil once said, "Man is born broken. He lives by mending. The grace of God is glue." Embracing my brokenness means not being surprised when I sin. It also means allowing my failures to be seen by others and knowing that it's okay to be broken because there's plenty of glue to go around.

Judas couldn't handle his brokenness and ran to hang himself, but Peter knew he was broken and ran for the empty tomb. How willing are you to accept God's glue?

REFLECT: *What are the obstacles that keep you from drawing near to the throne of grace?*

CAROLYN CARNEY

> *"I led them with cords of human kindness, with ties of love;*
> *I lifted the yoke from their neck and bent down to feed them."*

HOSEA 11:4

C. S. Lewis says that pride is "a spiritual cancer: it eats up the very possibility of love, or contentment, or even common sense." David had a kingdom, a palace and a relationship with God, but apparently these were not enough. He had to have a woman who did not belong to him. His pride squashed every ounce of common sense he had.

Often we indulge our lusts—sexual intimacies, overeating, pornography, casting judgment—in secret, mistakenly thinking that we're okay as long as no one finds out. In our pride we think ourselves sovereign over our secrets. David thought the same thing, but one sin led to another until his whole life began to unravel.

God knows the things that no one else knows about us, and he still bids us, "Come." He does not condemn or accuse but is gracious and merciful to us in our time of need. He responds to our pride with kindness, to our vain pursuits with the bread of life.

REFLECT: *What secret behaviors do you need to bring into the light, asking for God's forgiveness?*

CAROLYN CARNEY

FRIDAY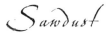

Let us throw off everything that hinders
and the sin that so easily entangles,
and let us run with perseverance the race marked out for us.

HEBREWS 12:1

I have a friend who is a carpenter. He said that if he works with wood in one room, it is very likely that he will find sawdust in a completely different room. He can't contain the sawdust because it is invisible while it travels, and as a result it shows up in the most unlikely of places.

Sin is a lot like sawdust. You can't keep it contained. And you can't hide it for long. Each "room" in our hearts is connected to the others in some way, and sin in one room will lead to sin in the other rooms. If our hearts are to be Christ's home, we must submit ourselves to the scrutiny of the Holy Spirit. We don't have to hide our "dust" from him. He comes to our homes not to judge but to clean.

REFLECT: *What aspects of your life feel especially out of control? How can God clean up these messes?*

ALEX GEE

SATURDAY/SUNDAY *Mirror, Mirror*

For now we see in a mirror, dimly, but . . .
then I will know fully, even as I have been fully known.

1 CORINTHIANS 13:12 NRSV

I don't know very many people who really enjoy looking at themselves in the mirror. Mirrors show us up; you can't hide from the imperfect reality of who you are.

But the mirror, as Paul says, offers only a dim reflection of ultimate reality. The true question for anyone following Jesus is not "Who am I?" but rather "Who am I becoming?"

If we follow Jesus, we are becoming fully who Jesus intends us to be. The image in the mirror is ephemeral. What is both eternal and most real is not how we feel about ourselves but who Jesus is making us to be.

PRAY: *Look in the mirror as you pray. Ask Jesus to help you recognize who you are becoming and to show you how to move toward that image.*

ALISON SIEWERT

M O N D A Y

The Family Room

> *"Is it not written, 'My house shall be called a house of prayer for all the nations'?*
> *But you have made it a den of robbers."*

MARK 11:17 NRSV

Jesus went to Jerusalem looking for a temple that included and prayed for all the nations of earth. What he found was more like an exclusive club, a clique that communicated it was closed, not open, to foreigners.

When Jesus ascended and left us the Holy Spirit, the people of God became a living temple. We are to be the place of prayer for all the nations, the welcome mat to the kingdom of God. But are we?

Who would feel comfortable in your house? Whom do you feel comfortable having in your house? If Jesus is in your home, certainly the nations will show up searching for him. And if Jesus is in your heart, surely you will search for the nations in prayer and mission.

PRAY: *Pray over a globe or world map, asking Jesus to help you develop active hope for those who have never heard of him.*

ALISON SIEWERT

TUESDAY *A New Identity*

"By your blood you ransomed for God
saints from every tribe and language and people and nation;
you have made them to be a kingdom."

REVELATION 5:9-10 NRSV

Jesus gives us a new identity. When we realize what he has accomplished for us by the shedding of his blood, we can no longer accept the usual definitions of who we are. I may continue to have a special affection for my ethnic heritage or the nation in which I have been raised. But from now on the only identity I can boast about is my identity in Jesus.

This new identity is not just an individual thing. It means that I now belong to a different kind of community. I have a new way of thinking about who is "my own kind." Tribespeople in Brazil, business folks in South Korea, mine workers in Africa, single parents in the cities of North America—all of these who have come to faith in Christ are now my kinfolk.

REFLECT: *Think about who your real "relatives" are in Christ. How should this affect the way you pray?*

RICHARD J. MOUW

Jonah and Me

But Jonah was greatly displeased and became angry.

JONAH 4:1

Often our preconceived notions of others distance us so much that we don't even give them a chance. Jonah didn't like the arrogant Ninevites. He knew if he preached they would repent. But he wanted them to be judged and was displeased when God relented and brought mercy instead.

When I first visited South Africa in 1990 I had no interest in meeting white people. I thought most of them were racist, and the few I met during those six weeks supported my hunch. However, later I met a white woman who helped bring conviction to my judging heart.

Emma took her speech therapy training into Baragwanath Hospital, the only hospital serving the two million blacks residing in Soweto. The conditions were appalling, waiting was excruciating, and pay was paltry. Certainly, Emma could have worked in a better place, but she knew this was where she should be. Becoming friends with her opened my eyes to see that I had judged an entire racial group just for the color of their skin.

R E F L E C T : *Who have you written off before you even knew him or her? How can you change your posture toward that person?*

CAROLYN CARNEY

Never Colorblind

> *After this I looked and there before me was a great multitude that no one could count,*
> *from every nation, tribe, people and language,*
> *standing before the throne and in front of the Lamb.*

REVELATION 7:9

My friends wound me with their kindness. "I don't think of you as Chinese American," they'll insist. "I just think of you as Greg Jao."

I know that they mean well. But can they know me well if they don't see the color of my skin or the shape of my eyes? If they don't hear the echoes of China in my thoughts or the whispers of an immigrant family's worries in my behavior? (Imagine a girlfriend whispering to me, "I don't think of you as a man. I just think of you as Greg.") I am not merely an individual. I belong to a people.

Thankfully, Jesus isn't colorblind. In heaven we find ethnic diversity celebrated and cultural differences preserved. In fact, the ethnic and cultural diversity highlights the glory of the One who sits on the throne.

JOURNAL: *How does your ethnic or cultural background shape who you are? How might God use it for his glory?*

GREG JAO

Why, God?

> *"My grace is sufficient for you,*
> *for my power is made perfect in weakness."*
>
> 2 CORINTHIANS 12:9

Tell me, how could a loving God let something like this happen?"

I hate that question! I can't answer it when tragedy hits in my own life, and I certainly can't answer it for anyone else. But as I look back over my most distressing experiences, I am able to see what I was blind to while I was in the midst of my distress: *I can trust God.* In my pain, God ministers to me at a much deeper level than when I am comfortable in my own self-sufficiency.

When we are floundering helplessly, our hearts cry out to God. In our distress, we turn to him for relief. But relief is not always his will for us. If we are to ask for the greatest good, we will ask first and foremost that God be glorified through our suffering. And to be able to witness God meeting the deepest needs of his people in their darkest hours does indeed bring glory to his name.

R E F L E C T : *Read Psalm 25 and find relief in remembering that the greatest good is that God be glorified.*

KAY MARSHALL STROM

The grace of the Lord Jesus Christ, and the love of God,
and the fellowship of the Holy Spirit be with you all.

2 CORINTHIANS 13:14

On Trinity Sunday we contemplate the wondrous mystery of the simultaneous "threeness" and "oneness" of our God. *The Book of Common Prayer* addresses the Father in this way: "With your co-eternal Son and Holy Spirit, you are one God, one Lord, in Trinity of Persons and in Unity of Being."

We cannot begin to fathom this theological conundrum here, but we can take heart from Paul's trinitarian benediction that closes 2 Corinthians. He prays a threefold blessing: the *grace* of Jesus whereby we gain undeserved spiritual wealth through his sacrifice; the *love* of the Father whereby we become daughters and sons through his unconditional adoption of us; the *communion* of the Spirit whereby we know an intimate Presence that also unites us in one family. This blessing, if we experience it, strengthens us so that we can give ourselves in serving others. It is multifaceted generosity from our multipersoned God!

REFLECT: *To whom can you be a blessing, a channel for the grace, love and communion of the Father, Son and Holy Spirit?*

BOBBY GROSS

M O N D A Y *The Back Porch*

> *Paul went to see them [Aquila and Priscilla],*
> *and because he was a tentmaker as they were, he stayed and worked with them.*

A C T S 1 8 : 2 - 3

The back porch inevitably becomes cluttered with the stuff of ordinary life. We leave dirty boots and sweaty shirts there after working in the garden. We varnish an old chair. Work clothes hang from rusty hooks and paint cans collect dust. A couple of white wicker chairs allow for quiet conversation with a neighbor.

Aquila and Priscilla were tentmakers, as was the apostle Paul. What brought them together was not simply their common faith; it was also their trade. They had the kind of relationship that uses the back porch, a room that connects one's home to the ordinary outside world. Paul accomplished more in his years of service to Christ than perhaps anyone else in the history of Christianity. Yet he practiced an ordinary trade too, and he enjoyed warm friendships with people like Aquila and Priscilla. He spent time on the back porch, learning how to love and serve God there.

J O U R N A L : *In what ways can you honor and serve Jesus in the ordinary, earthly duties of your life?*

GERALD L. SITTSER

Woman with a Lamp

> *But he wanted to justify himself, so he asked Jesus,*
> *"And who is my neighbor?"*

LUKE 10:29

Suppose you are a woman alone in a house along a remote stretch of road. It's a cold night with heavy snow falling. A strange car pulls into your driveway. A stranger gets out of the car. He raises the hood, but that could be a trick. Would you go outside to ask him what was wrong?

One woman did. The car was ours, and we were driving across Michigan. The woman came out of the house to ask if she could help. She got a light so my husband could see what he was doing, and in a few minutes her house was somewhere behind us in the darkness.

In the same situation, I don't know if I would have come out of the house. But to that woman, a stranded traveler was her neighbor, just as much as the person who lived a mile down the road.

A C T : *Keep your eyes open for someone who needs your care today.*

SANDY LARSEN

Open the Door

> *But Martha was distracted by all the preparations.*
>
> LUKE 10:40

The day after tomorrow, a group of international students will come to our house for lunch. Ten have signed up to come, which means we could have anywhere from eight to twenty. Student life is always fluid, and foreign students seem especially subject to sudden changes of plans.

Today, like Martha, I am very distracted. My preparations are not complete. I know a couple of the students, but most will be strangers. What will they think of my home? Will they like the food? What will they think of me?

What a waste of energy! It is not my job to have a perfect house or perfect food. I will do the best I can, but my main responsibility is to open the door—both the door to my home and the door to my heart—and let these dear people in. It is the Lord in and through me who will make them feel welcome, for the heart of God and the door to heaven are already open to them.

ACT: *With whom can you share hospitality this week, whether at your home or somewhere else?*

SANDY LARSEN

THURSDAY *The Least of These*

> *"Get up . . . take the child and his mother and escape to Egypt.*
> *Stay there until I tell you, for Herod is going to search for the child to kill him."*

MATTHEW 2:13

We rarely think of Jesus, the Lord of the universe, as a refugee. It seems sacrilegious almost. But the infant Jesus was taken away in the dark of night as his parents fled the terror of Herod. What might they have experienced there in a foreign land? Dangerous travel, poverty, xenophobia, unemployment, hunger, homelessness, disease, uncertainty, loneliness, language barriers. The Gospel writers are silent about who helped Jesus' family, but certainly someone did.

There are approximately thirty-five million refugees in the world today. Many have fled from political crises. What would it mean for the church to show hospitality?

Jesus said, "Just as you did it to one of the least of these who are members of my family you did it to me" (see Matthew 25:40). At one time in his life, he was the "least of these," looked after by strangers in a foreign land. Serving the least means that we serve Jesus.

ACT: *Check with your church about opportunities to serve the immigrant population or other communities struggling to get by in your area.*

CAROLYN CARNEY

FRIDAY

Presenting Jesus to the World

Someone will say, "You have faith; I have deeds."
Show me your faith without deeds, and I will show you my faith by what I do.

JAMES 2:18

Friedrich Nietzsche, the atheistic philosopher, allegedly stated, "Jesus' disciples will need to look more saved if I am to believe in their Savior." Nietzsche used the poor witness of some Christians as his excuse for not believing, but he makes a good point: the world is looking for followers of Christ who look like Jesus. The world looks at believers not only for right belief but also for a distinctive Christlike lifestyle, a faith expressed through action. They are saying, "Show me your faith by the way you live and serve in this hurting world."

Service exemplifies the way Christianity is supposed to be lived. Believers who visibly and actively serve present Jesus to a watching world.

REFLECT: *What practical acts of service can you perform in the name of Jesus that will show your friends and neighbors that you are a follower of Jesus Christ?*

RICK EZELL

Scratch~Proofing

Love your neighbor as yourself.

LEVITICUS 19:18.

My cats are adorable, don't get me wrong, but there are times that I think they're demon-possessed.

I have indoor cats, which means I don't let them roam the neighborhood. Not everyone makes the same decision regarding their cats, and occasionally a cat will wander into our yard. My cats see this neighbor and react with hisses, then growls, then moans, then wails, then noises I'd never heard before and can't bring myself to describe. They claw at the windows and then turn on one another. By the time the outdoor cat leaves, my cats are as inconsolable as they have been inhospitable.

If they behaved more like I do, my cats wouldn't get so worked up. They'd simply ignore their neighbors until they went away.

Hmm. Perhaps my posture toward my neighbor should be something other than hostility or indifference. Perhaps I should try love.

ACT: *Introduce yourself to someone on the periphery of your life.*

DAVID A. ZIMMERMAN

M O N D A Y

The Attic

> *Not only was the Teacher wise,*
> *but also he imparted knowledge to the people.*

E C C L E S I A S T E S   1 2 : 9

Ask anyone to make a list of the most important people in his or her life, and you are sure to find the name of a teacher on it. You will on my list. Mrs. Eckert is right at the top. Through her passion for great literature, she taught me to love words. She took my silly little melodramatic attempt at an original story and, with tears in her eyes, declared that one day I really would be a writer. Because she believed in me, I began to believe in myself. If Mrs. Eckert said so, it had to be true!

Mrs. Eckert also taught me to trust God through the hardest of times. By her words, but even more by how she acted when her husband died suddenly, and then when her blind father came to live with her and soon after also died. Mrs. Eckert taught me by allowing me to see how her life agreed with her words.

JOURNAL: *Who are some of the people in your history who modeled a life of faith for you? How has your life reflected their influence?*

KAY MARSHALL STROM

An Undergirding of Prayer

The prayer of a righteous man is powerful and effective.

JAMES 5:16

A college senior and a fairly new Christian, I left for my final semester on an internship in Detroit without acquaintances or housing. Then I remembered Kevin, a guy I'd met briefly on campus who'd moved to Motown, and I made arrangements to meet with him. Over dinner I unloaded my housing woes. He got quiet. "I attend this little church. The pastor rents a basement apartment . . ." Twelve hours after meeting the pastor and his family I unpacked my belongings.

Another time Kevin said, "I go to this singles' group at another church. Wanna come?" God seemed to be steering, so I hopped in and ended up meshing with the pastor's daughter, Beth. She began tutoring me in spiritual things, and her family adopted me. Twenty years later, Pastor Whiz and his lovely wife Lois still pray for me, cheering over joys and weeping over needs. I cannot imagine life without that constant undergirding. I'll e-mail them right now and thank them for their faithful lives. And I'm thanking God for Kevin, wherever he is.

PRAY: *Recall and thank God for people who served you in times of need.*

JANE RUBIETTA

The Choice

> *If you forgive anyone, I also forgive him.*
>
> 2 CORINTHIANS 2:10

Think about the one person in your life you don't like to think about—the person who has hurt you most deeply. Maybe the hurt has come recently, or maybe it happened years ago. Maybe you live with the pain every day.

The apostle Paul had a person in his life like that, a man who claimed to love Paul but who ended up cutting his heart to shreds. The man finally repented, but only after the community of believers rebuked him. He never apologized directly to Paul.

Paul thought everything about that man that you have thought about the person in your life. He felt anger and betrayal and revenge, but in the end, he decided to do just one thing: he made the choice to forgive.

Carrying bitterness around in our hearts just isn't worth it. We can't wait until we have warm feelings about the other person, because forgiveness is a choice not a feeling. The rest of the work is up to God.

REFLECT: *What offense in your memory has been hardest for you to forgive?*

DOUGLAS CONNELLY

Storing Memories

> *We will not hide them from their children;*
> *we will tell the next generation the praiseworthy deeds of the LORD,*
> *his power, and the wonders he has done.*

PSALM 78:4

André Malraux, the French writer-politician, has said, "One day it will be realized that men are distinguishable from one another as much by the forms their memories take as by their characters." What a remarkable observance!

What happens when we rummage around in the boxes of memory in the attic of our mind? When the scrapbooks spill their contents, do we respond with bitterness, anger, resentment, self-flagellation? Or are the memories of all the wounds of the past being transformed? Can we say about that old photo of personal folly, "I erred but God taught me grace"?

When the memories spill out of their containers, are we grateful? If gratitude doesn't light the garret of the soul, doesn't it say something about unfinished cleaning that still needs to be accomplished? And what memories will we leave to the generations who come to stack and sort and catalog after us?

REFLECT: *Are you distinguishable from others as much by the quality of your memories as by your character?*

KAREN MAINS

The Morals of Our Stories

In his heart a man plans his course,
but the LORD determines his steps.

PROVERBS 16:9

My parents stored my comic books for me for years, until I finally packed them up and brought them home. Then I read them again.

In an instant the story lines came back to me: good guys who tried to be good, bad guys who in many cases thought they were being good. Who knew life could be full of such moral confusion?

The years have taught me that, in reality, life is plenty full of moral confusion. Many times I've done what I thought was the right thing only to cause hurt to people I cared about. Many times I've convinced myself I was doing the right thing while I pursued my advantage at the expense of someone else. Many times it seems I've done the right thing only by sheer accident.

Fortunately, we are shepherded by a moral God who defines the good for us. Comic books may tell fantasy stories of moral ambiguity, but God writes our stories, and he tells us the truth.

JOURNAL: *What, outside your faith, shaped your moral sense as a child? How do you reconcile moments of moral confusion today?*

DAVID A. ZIMMERMAN

Life with Christ

> *[God] grant . . . that Christ may dwell in your hearts through faith.*
>
> EPHESIANS 3:16-17

Without question one of the most remarkable Christian doctrines is that Jesus Christ himself, through the Holy Spirit, will enter a heart, settle down and be at home there. Christ will live in any human heart that welcomes him.

I will never forget the evening I invited him into my heart. He came into the darkness of my heart and turned on the light. He built a fire in the cold hearth and banished the chill. He started music where there had been stillness and harmony where there had been discord. He filled the emptiness with his own loving fellowship. I have never regretted opening the door to Christ, and I never will.

REFLECT: *Think back on your earliest memories of life with Christ. How did the presence of Christ change your life? Beyond flash or spectacle, what was it like to know that God had settled in with you?*

ROBERT BOYD MUNGER

M O N D A Y *Transferring the Title*

> *Do you not know that your body is a temple of the Holy Spirit,*
> *who is in you, whom you have received from God?*
> *You are not your own; you were bought at a price.*

1 CORINTHIANS 6:19-20

A sign hangs by our front door bearing the single word *Rehoboth*, which is the Hebrew for "room" (Genesis 26:22). One day I answered the doorbell to greet a phone company representative who was going door-to-door to drum up business. She asked if I was Mrs. Johnson, and I said that the Johnsons didn't live there anymore. I watched in confusion, then in amusement, as she crossed out *Johnson* on her clipboard and began to diligently copy the name on our sign: R-E-H-O-B . . . I suppose I could have let the mistake stand—and counted how many telemarketing calls we got for "Mr. and Mrs. Rehoboth"— but I explained that *Rehoboth* was a Bible reference, not our last name!

The door to a Christian's inner life should bear a sign with the name of Christ on it. The previous tenant is gone. Christ is now the owner of the house.

REFLECT: *If a sign proclaimed the owner of your heart, what name would be there?*

SANDY LARSEN

Just Do It!

Test me, O LORD, and try me, examine my heart and my mind. . . .
I lead a blameless life.

PSALM 26:2, 11

There comes a point where you've just had enough. You are going to put aside the immature behavior that has dogged your life; you are going to deal with an area of disobedience once and for all. This is where you draw the line and you aren't looking back.

That's where David was when he wrote Psalm 26. He stood up and said, "I lead a blameless life." David wasn't claiming to be sinless. Being blameless means that your sin is handled correctly before God and before others. David wanted everyone to know that the intent of his heart was to do the will of God.

Have you had enough of your half-hearted commitment to the Lord? Are you ready to take a stand in your home, in your church, in your workplace, with your friends? Write a psalm of your own. Declare to God and to others where your priorities lie. Determine that your life will never be the same again.

PRAY: *Test me, God. Examine my heart and my mind.*

DOUGLAS CONNELLY

/ Resolve

> *"We will never find any basis for charges against this man Daniel*
> *unless it has something to do with the law of his God."*

DANIEL 6:5

Daniel in the lions' den has always been one of my favorite Bible stories. Even as a kid, I was impressed by the fact that Daniel was not tossed in with hungry lions for being bad. He was tossed in for being godly.

All the Sunday school pictures of Daniel in the lions' den show him to be a man about forty years old. The fact is that Daniel was in his eighties when he landed on the lions' lunch menu. For more than seventy years he had survived in Babylon, and the secret of his spiritual survival is found in six words in Daniel 1:8: "Daniel resolved not to defile himself."

That is still the requirement for spiritual survival in a secular world: determination to stand true to God no matter what the cost. Daniel set his mind to live for God. That made the choices very clear when the difficult challenges came.

R E F L E C T : *Where will you stand when the test of your obedience to God comes?*

DOUGLAS CONNELLY

Heart of Flesh

"I will give you a new heart and put a new spirit in you;
I will remove from you your heart of stone and give you a heart of flesh."

EZEKIEL 36:26

After the high surf the previous day, rocks littered the shore. Holes pock-marked the stones where water had corroded their surfaces, and I remembered our family Scripture, Ezekiel 36:26. God promised to replace my heart of stone with a heart of flesh, and while I waited for him to change my circumstances, he waited for me to let him drill into that stone so his softness, his heart, could flow through me. Bit by bit, instance by instance, I let tiny streams of God's Spirit work out the stone.

The holes in the stones on the beach were a picture of my own heart as I let God have his way with me, opening myself to whatever he wanted to do in me, in our family. Whatever he wanted: that's a strong release of all the con-trolling demands I'd made for improvement, perfection, happiness. Whatever God wants to do is better than anything I could dream up or demand.

JOURNAL: *What's your immediate reaction to the idea of committing yourself to "whatever God wants to do"? Reflect on how you have surrendered yourself to God.*

JANE RUBIETTA

Transformed

> *"You are Simon son of John. You will be called Cephas"*
> *(which, when translated, is Peter).*

JOHN 1:42

Jesus sees us not simply as we are but also as what we will become. When he met Simon the first time, Jesus met a man who was moody, wavering—a man with no real direction in life. But Jesus also saw what Simon could and would become. "You will be called 'Rock'!"

Shifting Simon would one day plant his feet firmly on the conviction that Jesus was Lord and God. It wouldn't happen overnight. He would stumble and fall and fail along the way. But in time, Simon would become Peter—and not just in name, but in character.

I spend a lot of time looking only at what I am. Not nearly enough energy is focused on what Jesus is making me. The good news is that we don't have to be the people we are today for the rest of our lives. We can be changed by Jesus' transforming power.

PRAY: *Make me more rocklike, Lord, more like you.*

DOUGLAS CONNELLY

No Ballyhoo

> *Do not conform any longer to the pattern of this world,*
> *but be transformed by the renewing of your mind.*
> *Then you will be able to test and approve what God's will is—*
> *his good, pleasing and perfect will.*

ROMANS 12:2

From two rooms away I heard the caller's bright, cheerful voice. I reached the phone and listened to the message—a recorded pitch for something or other. Even on a recording of a recording, the voice rang with enthusiasm. Whatever that person was offering me was the greatest deal in the world.

Every new advertisement promises something exceptional, superior, new and more advanced than anything else I could buy. Compared with the lavish promises of such ads, Paul sounds feeble and bland: "good, pleasing and perfect." Why didn't the Holy Spirit have Paul write that God's will is "stupendous, thrilling and colossal"?

Perhaps the will of God is not a product to acquire but a mandate to obey.

REFLECT: *How have you found God's will to be good, pleasing and perfect? Praise him for revealing his will to humanity.*

SANDY LARSEN

Summer

M O N D A Y

Making Your Heart a Home

"If anyone hears my voice and opens the door,
I will come in and eat with him, and he with me."

REVELATION 3:20

Home is the place where I can be myself and find real rest. "Jesus is the head of my house," I've always claimed. But I wonder if my heart feels like a place of rest for him. Or have I allowed worry, fear, worldly pleasures and distractions to clutter his dwelling place?

I haven't fully mastered the art of welcoming Christ every moment of my day. To be honest, some days I see him as unexpected company arriving at the most inopportune time. I'm often embarrassed by the condition of my heart when I sense his nearness. But even in my embarrassment, he never wants to leave and always asks to stay and lend a hand.

So, such as it is, I say, "Welcome home, Lord."

REFLECT: *How would you describe the condition of your heart today? Is it a place of rest for your Lord?*

MARSHA CROCKETT

Under the Influence

> *Do not get drunk on wine, which leads to debauchery.*
> *Instead, be filled with the Spirit.*

EPHESIANS 5:18

In Ephesians 5:18 the apostle Paul draws a contrast between someone who is filled with alcohol and someone who is filled with the Spirit. A person who is filled with alcohol is controlled by the alcohol. Its presence and power have overridden his normal abilities. In the same way, having the fullness of the Spirit can be defined as being controlled by the Spirit's presence and power. The Holy Spirit possesses the believer's mind and heart—his or her very being.

We often say that someone is "under the influence" of alcohol, and in some ways that is also what it is like when we are filled with the Spirit. We are "under the influence" of the Spirit. Instead of doing things only with our own strength or ability, the Spirit empowers us. Instead of doing only what we want to do, we are guided by the Spirit.

REFLECT: *What is (and what is not) under the influence of the Spirit in your life?*

RICK EZELL

Not My Will

> *"My Father, if it is possible, may this cup be taken from me.*
> *Yet not as I will, but as you will."*

MATTHEW 26:39

How wonderful it is to bow to God in prayer, praising him for who he is. How blessed to kneel down in thanksgiving, recalling his gracious mercies and the petitions he has answered. What a comfort to be able to come before him with the desires of our hearts and to intercede on behalf of others who are in need of God's hand in their lives. But one part of prayer is hard—so hard that many times we mumble it insincerely or skip over it altogether.

When things are going well, it's easy to think of ourselves as obedient to God's will. But when something takes a sharp turn in a direction we don't like, then it's not as easy to trust God. That's the time when we most need to do what Jesus did: fall on our faces and pray, "Not as I will, but as you will."

JOURNAL: *Recall a time when you had a hard time following God's will in a particular situation. What made it so hard? How can you guard against that attitude toward God?*

KAY MARSHALL STROM

Tongue Control

Do not grieve the Holy Spirit of God.

EPHESIANS 4:30

One day I was talking with my father, and I heard the familiar sharp, ugly tone in my voice as I spoke with him, this most gentle of men. The Holy Spirit sliced my mind with Ephesians 4:29: "Do not let any unwholesome talk come out of your mouths, but only what is helpful for building others up according to their needs."

Immediately I gave up tongue control to God and asked my dad's forgiveness for my words—something unheard of in my mouthy world. I headed home with a new awareness that in spite of my mouth, my dad loved me, just like my heavenly Father did.

REFLECT: *Where have your words gotten in the way of relationships? What does it take for God to help bring your mouth under control?*

JANE RUBIETTA

God's Requirements

What does the LORD require of you?
To act justly and to love mercy and to walk humbly with your God.

MICAH 6:8

The summer when I was fourteen years old, I decided to make a dramatic display of my spirituality: I would read through the entire Bible before school started in the fall. I got as far as Micah 6, and what I read there stopped me in my tracks. The prophet cried out to God, "What can I give you? Huge sacrifices? Thousands of rams? Ten thousand rivers of oil? Do you demand the ultimate sacrifice of me—my firstborn child?" (see Micah 6:6-7). God's response to the prophet gave me my first glimpse of who God is. He expects three things from those who would follow him: See that justice is done, be merciful and humbly obey him. If God's children would practice these three things, they would change the course of history.

A C T : *Keep an eye out today for ways you can stand for justice and practice mercy. Ask God to show you the way of humility in those circumstances.*

KAY MARSHALL STROM

Extending Grace

> *[Love] always protects, always trusts,*
> *always hopes, always perseveres.*

1 CORINTHIANS 13:7

I'm really angry! What started out as a minor disagreement has gotten out of hand, and I'm convinced that it's my husband's fault! Oh, I know I'm not always right, and when I'm wrong, I'm willing to apologize. But this time I'm right, so I'm not about to back down! Why should I? And if he thinks I will, he can just . . .

I hate it when our home is filled with tension and strife. How much sweeter it is when love and peace rule. There is a way to move through the strife-ridden tension and get back to the loving peace we both long for, but it requires a step that is awfully hard for me to take. I have to extend grace to my husband. Even when I don't feel like it. Even when I am certain I am justified in my anger.

If I want to be like Jesus, then to extend grace must become my way of life. And where better to begin than at home?

ACT: *Is there someone to whom you need to extend grace? What specific thing can you do to reach out to that person?*

KAY MARSHALL STROM

MONDAY

The Study

Great are the works of the LORD;
they are pondered by all who delight in them.

PSALM 111:2

The psalmist came to understand God through study. This kind of study, however, is not the rote, dry exercise of preparing for exams that elicits groans from students. The works of God are studied by those who delight in them and delighted in by those who study them.

The Lord creates so that he can be known. He has made his wonders in order that we will remember him. God wants us to find him, to know what he is like and how he works in the world.

We are shaped by what we see as we study God's works in the Word and the world. God's design and his interpretation of his own work build a frame of reference for us to perceive and enjoy all of the life he gives us. Through our study, God's perspective becomes ours—and that's nothing to groan at.

JOURNAL: *Tonight write down three ways you've seen God work; reread them in the morning, then write down God's work in a Scripture passage; reread your notes before you go to sleep.*

ALISON SIEWERT

Bring the Books

When you come, bring the cloak that I left with Carpus at Troas,
and my scrolls, especially the parchments.

2 TIMOTHY 4:13

In his final letter the apostle Paul made an unusual request of his friend Timothy. Paul was in prison, facing his last days on earth, and he couldn't imagine facing long, lonely days without books to read.

Paul never stopped learning. He could have been excused from study at this point. He was getting up in years. At any moment the executioner could show up and his life would end. There were no more preaching journeys to plan, no more sermons to prepare. Yet he was determined to keep stretching.

It's easy to think that we've mastered our jobs. We may even think that we've gained significant knowledge of the Bible and spiritual truth. The committed Christian, however, is never satisfied with the status quo. The growing Christian never stops learning. Where does that leave you? Are you feeding your spirit with God's truth and challenging your mind and heart with good books? If you were sitting in a prison cell, what would you ask for?

A C T : *Ask a pastor or spiritual advisor for some suggested books to read.*

DOUGLAS CONNELLY

Christianity for Dummies?

Instruct a wise man and he will be wiser still;
teach a righteous man and he will add to his learning.

PROVERBS 9:9

At some stage in my rebellious past, I scoffed at anyone who took their faith *too* seriously. There were lots of religious ideas in the world. Why get too straight-laced about any one of them, especially one as simplistic as the Christian faith? Christianity was for dummies, people who hadn't yet learned how to think.

God must have laughed at me. Then he introduced me to a group of creative, fun-loving, learned and godly women. And he surrounded me with Christian scholars who challenged my mind and my heart. Eventually he gave me a chance to study ancient scholars of the faith: Augustine, Gregory the Great, Anselm, Aquinas and later Luther, Calvin, Wesley and Edwards. There wasn't an academic slouch in the lot.

Sure, the Christian faith is simple enough for a child to understand—and believe. But it is also complex enough to intrigue the mind for all of a lifetime.

A C T : *Select a challenging Christian book, perhaps one from one of the great minds of our past. Allow it to stretch your mind and your faith.*

CAROLYN NYSTROM

Knowing the Word

*"You diligently study the Scriptures because you think that
by them you possess eternal life;
These are the Scriptures that testify about me,
yet you refuse to come to me."*

JOHN 5:39-40

We tend to look down on the Pharisees and scribes of Jesus' day, but in reality they were committed to knowing and following God's Word.

How often I have studied Scripture in an effort to know it well without giving myself to knowing Jesus well. It's possible for us to find Jesus making us coffee in the kitchen or waiting for us in the living room, all while we're holed up in the study, knowing more stuff.

We must live with Jesus. It is not enough to visit him occasionally. To know "the truth" is not to know a set of propositions but to know a person.

REFLECT: *What action do you need to take to get out of the study and spend time with Jesus personally? How can Jesus join you in your study of Scripture?*

ALISON SIEWERT

Words of Honey

[Your words, God,]
are more precious than gold . . .
sweeter than honey.

PSALM 19:10

I was interviewing women in an underground church in China for *Daughters of Hope,* a book on the persecuted church, when a tiny old lady grabbed a pencil and paper and looked up at me expectantly. "What does she want?" I asked the interpreter.

"She is waiting for you to recite from the Bible so she can copy it down and keep it," the interpreter told me. "It is very difficult for us to get Bibles here—especially the book of Romans. Could you recite a chapter or two from the book of Romans for us?"

A chapter or two? I didn't know any chapters of Romans by memory, even though Romans 8 is my favorite part of the Bible.

When I got home, I began memorizing Scripture—and I started with Romans 8. The next time someone asks, I'll be ready!

JOURNAL: *What Scripture passage would you like to have tucked away in your heart? Copy it into a notebook you can carry with you as you work at committing it to memory.*

KAY MARSHALL STROM

> *Resist the devil, and he will flee from you.*
>
> JAMES 4:7

Oscar Wilde was right when he said, "I can resist everything except temptation." Nowhere in Scripture are we told to resist temptation. If victory is to be secured, we must fight the devil with uncompromising resolve and stand firm with uncommon valor.

Jesus did. Just as quickly as Satan hurled his fiery temptations, Jesus picked them up and threw them back in his face—immediately, decisively, defiantly. Jesus resisted the devil. He did not ignore the devil. He did not argue theology with the devil. He did not negotiate with the devil. Instead, he answered him sharply. Digging in his heels, he countered the devil's offensive attack.

The word *resist* is a military word that means "to stop or hinder the progress of an adversary." In this context it means to refrain from a temptation. If we are to resist Satan, we must stop his attempts to destroy us before we are harmed.

JOURNAL: *How are you affected by temptation? What resources can you draw on to help you resist it when it comes?*

RICK EZELL

M O N D A Y

The Dining Room

He brought me to the banqueting house.

SONG OF SONGS 2:4 NRSV

M*y Heart—Christ's Home* was the first Christian book I ever owned. I had just come to believe in Jesus (after seventeen years as a Buddhist), and I wanted him to clean up my messes. But when I ventured into the "dining room," my understanding of what being a Christian meant did a 180-degree spin. All my current appetites and desires were questioned and challenged. I had no idea that following Jesus meant a new diet consisting of a different view on money, fame and fortune—three irresistible entrées up until then. Neither had anyone told me that my favorite sins were not good for my soul.

C. S. Lewis wrote in *Mere Christianity*, "Imagine yourself as a living house. God comes in to rebuild that house. . . . You thought you were going to be made into a decent little cottage; but he is building up a palace. He intends to come and live in it himself."

I needed to stock this palace with food fit for a king, which meant that my diet needed to change.

JOURNAL: *What appetites and desires do you bring into your relationship with Jesus? How might those appetites and desires be adapted for your life in God's palace?*

PAUL TOKUNAGA

TUESDAY

"I have food to eat that you know nothing about."

JOHN 4:32

From Genesis to Revelation God is pictured as a caring Father who feeds his people. But there is more. He does not feed us merely with the good things he has made; he feeds us his very self. This other "bread"—the Word of God himself—we must *learn* to eat. Our whole lives consist of learning what he meant when he said, "I have food to eat that you know nothing about."

Mother Teresa reportedly said, "In India people are dying of physical starvation. In America people are dying of emotional starvation." In other words, a spiritual hunger exists that cannot be quenched by physical food. Jesus bids us to his feast that binds hungry sinners together and links us to the one who alone can feed our souls.

PRAY: *Let the sensation of hunger pangs today remind you to thank God for feeding us with his Word.*

RICK EZELL

Preparing for the Competition

Everyone who competes in the games goes into strict training.

1 CORINTHIANS 9:25

Imagine being an athlete training for the Olympic trials. Each day starts at the crack of dawn with a rigorous workout that involves stretching muscles, building endurance and perfecting technique. Yet after long hours of sweat, pain and pushing your body to the limit, the regimen is not complete. A crucial part of the training program is nutrition. A healthy, well-balanced meal plan is essential for providing strength and energy to your body. For the serious competitor, there is no room for excess weight caused by junk food.

We too must be careful not to become bogged down by excess weight caused by spiritual "junk food." Sins such as materialism, lust, jealousy, gossip, gluttony, racism and so on, weigh us down and disqualify us from serving the Lord. Just as the athlete cannot win the competition if he does not control what he eats, neither can we do the will of God when we do not practice restraint over worldly appetites.

PRAY: *Ask God to help you steer your hunger to things that are worthy of his table.*

RAYMOND M. CAUSEY

Starving

> *"My gauntness rises up and testifies against me."*
>
> JOB 16:8

My son and I crowded onto the only available bench outside the lab, awaiting routine tests. On the opposite bench, someone was curled in a ball, small enough to be a child. We overheard a man at the registration desk saying, "Her stomach hurts. She needs a doctor."

A moan escaped from the crumpled body. The receptionist, who had said, "I'm sorry, but we can't get you in today," relented with a panicked look and hustled over with a wheelchair. The man gingerly picked up his wife and placed her in the chair. Her arms hung uselessly. Clothes draped her frame like fabric on a stick. My heart aching, I said, "Zak, I think she is starving to death."

How many times have I been dying because I haven't eaten what nourishes my soul? How often have I gotten swept into work and busyness, becoming a perpetually fasting marathon runner? I don't want to live this way, and so I turn to the Bible open on my desk, hungry for food to fuel my heart.

REFLECT: *When do you fast in order to keep moving? What happens in your soul when you choose work over God?*

JANE RUBIETTA

Food for Life

> *"Listen, listen to me, and eat what is good,*
> *and your soul will delight in the richest of fare."*

ISAIAH 55:2

If you like pizza, Chicago is a great place to be. There are two different restaurants that I particularly like with very different styles of pizza. Roundheads' is thin-crust, chewy not crispy, with a nice amount of cheese. The grease puddles a bit, but not too much. The pizza is cut into small squares, so it's hard to keep count of how much you've eaten.

Giordano's pizza, however, is my passion. Giordano's features a thick-crust pizza with a pile of cheese that requires a knife to cut through it, and the sauce comes on top. It is always worth the forty-minute wait while they make it, and two slices will leave you feeling stuffed.

Food sustains us. Our bodies require it. In the same way, our souls require sustenance, and we have a choice whether to consume something that is simply good or something that will fill us completely. While I may enjoy the occasional small, greasy square, I cannot consume that day after day. I need the Giordano's experience.

REFLECT: *How can you take the time to fill yourself with God today?*

CINDY BUNCH

When God Says No

Three different times I begged God to make me well again.
Each time he said, "No."

2 CORINTHIANS 12:8-9 LB

No is an ugly word. It is terribly troubling to believers when it comes from a God who promises to answer prayer and do great things.

Faith creates problems for us. To believe in a sovereign God who can heal the sick, raise the dead, annihilate the devil and launder the earth clean of every blight forces us to face the question: "If he can, why doesn't he? Why doesn't God just release his power and heal all the hurts? I would, if I were God."

But we are not God. And healing sometimes is not God's plan, nor his way. Instead he offers us his presence, which offers the greatest comfort and healing of all.

JOURNAL: *Recall a time you were troubled by God's "No." In what ways did his presence comfort you?*

RICK EZELL

M O N D A Y   *The Living Room*

In the morning, O LORD, you hear my voice;
in the morning I lay my requests before you and wait in expectation.

PSALM 5:3

Are you a morning person? If you are, good for you. I'm not. I am amazed at people who get up at 5:00 a.m. to read their Bibles and pray. I am amazed at people who can get up at 5:00 a.m. to do *anything.*

If early morning is not the best devotional time for you, don't feel guilty. Half-asleep Bible reading and prayer do not do much for your spirit. God knows your personal "clock," and he understands that evening—or noon, or some other time—may be better. The goal is to establish a regular habit. And if we forget, we don't have to wait twenty-four hours to reconnect with the Lord. He is always there, and any time is the right time to call on him.

ACT: *Have you found the best time of day or night to be alone with God, to read the Scriptures and pray? Try different times until devotions are a consistent part of your daily schedule.*

SANDY LARSEN

Since, then, you have been raised with Christ,
set your hearts on things above,
where Christ is seated at the right hand of God.

COLOSSIANS 3:1

I wanted to pray. I longed to pray. But my mind wandered worse than a toddler in a toy store. A list helped, but soon I wondered, *Why not just lay this sheet of paper before God? He already has it memorized from all my listing.*

Then when I was in a bookstore in Spain, I spotted a knobby ring with a cross sticking up from it. "A prayer ring," the clerk said. I bought it for one euro. Wearing the ring, my thumb pressing one of the knobs, I pray for a person, then shift knobs. Somehow this tactile tool focuses me. Ten knobs later, I have prayed for some time, covering family members, events and other things God highlighted.

I love this tool. When I use it, my soul is refreshed, loved ones are kept before him, and I feel as though I am helping God's kingdom come—to my heart and to others'.

REFLECT: *What helps focus your prayers? How can you move your heart back to God's throughout the day?*

JANE RUBIETTA

A New Perspective

> *After this I looked and there before me*
> *was a great multitude that no one could count,*
> *from every nation, tribe, people and language,*
> *standing before the throne and in front of the Lamb.*

REVELATION 7:9

Lon and Leah Knival are working in the Iteri tribe in Papua New Guinea. When translating the parable of the sower, they were looking for the best word for "good soil," so their language guide took them to a place and showed them deep, rich soil that had formed through the decay of the best trees. It was "mulchy" soil. In that tribe, a heart made of good soil would most closely resemble a compost pile!

Looking at God's Word through different eyes can make your quiet times come alive again. Learning a psalm in American Sign Language, marking up a Bible to give to my sixteen-year-old son or even simply reading a different Bible translation are a few ways God woke up my quiet time. How can you renew *your* perspective?

A C T : *Need a new point of view? Try a different translation; attend a worship service of another culture, or just of another age group!*

PAM FARREL

As Natural As Breathing

Pray continually.

1 THESSALONIANS 5:17

The Desert Fathers paid attention to the natural rhythms of breathing and turned them into prayer. In an effort to pray unceasingly they would use "breath prayers" in which the inhalation was one part of the prayer and the exhalation was the completion of the thought. The prayer would often hone in on a vital aspect of that person's spiritual life and was an expression of his intimacy with God.

Last year on my sabbatical I used a breath prayer as I lit a floating candle in a glass holder. I prayed, "Lord, you are all around me; you uphold me" on my inhale. My exhalation was, "The light of Christ is in me." For my whole life I'd struggled to recognize Christ's presence within me, yet I continued to live a very public Christian life as a minister. So this prayer was a deeply personal expression of my faith journey.

I prayed this way throughout the day as I drove to the store, gardened, cleaned house, cooked meals, walked and waited. It became for me as natural as breathing.

PRAY: *Come up with your own breath prayer to address your current need in your faith walk.*

CAROLYN CARNEY

Our Father in Heaven

> *We do not know what we ought to pray for,*
> *but the Spirit himself intercedes for us with groans*
> *that words cannot express.*

ROMANS 8:26

When I was in Korea, I was invited to attend a church's daily prayer meeting. It met in the sanctuary—at 4:30 a.m.! At the appointed hour, my interpreter and I stumbled into the totally dark room. For an hour and a half we sat in the dark listening to impassioned prayers on behalf of believers around the world—prayers for strength, for wisdom, for protection, for courage to remain steadfast in the faith, for a spirit of forgiveness, for unity in the Spirit.

Later I asked, "Why is the room so dark? Couldn't you turn on the lights?"

"Oh, no!" my interpreter answered. "Then someone might be tempted to come to receive praise for getting up so early. We only want those to come who really want to pray. God knows, and their prayers are the ones he hears."

PRAY: *Intercede on behalf of the church around the world. Not sure how to pray? Remember, you have an intercessor too!*

KAY MARSHALL STROM

Look! Listen!

Peter and his companions were very sleepy,
but when they became fully awake, they saw his glory.

LUKE 9 : 32

Jesus once climbed a mountain to find a place to pray. He took three friends with him, as he often did. Apparently, they were nonchalant, nodding off as he knelt to pray. They nearly missed seeing Jesus dazzlingly "changed" and in conversation with Moses and Elijah!

At this time of year the church remembers the transfiguration. We remember that every day Jesus invites us to join in what he is doing. That prayer is never a routine exercise but always an encounter with "the majestic glory." We should pray with eyes open, paying attention, *looking*. Maybe then, like Peter, we will be "eyewitnesses of his majesty" (see 2 Peter 1:16-18) and hearers of the voice from heaven—and thus changed ourselves.

REFLECT: *Where might Jesus take you today? What can you do to stay alert to what he has for you?*

BOBBY GROSS

MONDAY *The Workroom*

> *The one who calls you is faithful and he will do it.*
>
> 1 THESSALONIANS 5:24

In the dream, I moved through a room that turned into an office. The office kept expanding, displaying stocked bookshelves, equipment, plentiful office supplies, a desk and a chair. The glow of discovery lit me from within; all this was here, and I hadn't known it?

When I woke up, the truth dawned on me: God was inviting me to act on the dream of writing, on the calling to use my gifts for his kingdom, and he was providing me with all the tools I could possibly use. Publication wasn't assured by the dream—it would take work to trust God's calling and begin to develop my writing—but I strongly sensed God's enabling. No longer could I excuse my lack of honing with comparison: "I can't write like so-and-so; I won't write at all." God had given me everything necessary for my unique calling, and he would be responsible for making things happen. I just had to write and submit. And rewrite. And resubmit.

JOURNAL: *What are your excuses for avoiding your calling? How can you stop excusing and begin trusting—and acting?*

JANE RUBIETTA

The Unimportant Parts

In Christ we who are many form one body,
and each member belongs to all the others.

ROMANS 12:5

A friend of mine used to complain that all the other members of the body of Christ got to be beautiful body parts, like eyes. Or useful parts, like hands. Or important parts, like the heart. "All I am is a toe!" she would say.

She always got a laugh out of me—until the day I was helping my husband paint the exterior trim on our house and I dropped a brick on my toe. Suddenly that toe was the most important part of my entire body! I didn't give a single thought to my beautiful eyes or my useful hands or my important heart. In fact, all those other parts focused their attention on my hurting toe too.

In our human bodies, there are no unimportant parts. How much truer that is in the body of Christ.

REFLECT: *What special gifts have you been given? How are you using them for the good of the rest of Christ's body?*

KAY MARSHALL STROM

WEDNESDAY   *Specific Gifts*

> *Each one should use whatever gift he has received to serve others,*
> *faithfully administering God's grace in its various forms.*

1 PETER 4:10

I believe that our church pianist has the spiritual gift of accompaniment. I've never found that gift in any list in the Scriptures, but the idea must be there. When he accompanies a singer who is a little shaky, he must know he is a better piano player than the soloist is a singer, yet his playing never outshines the singing. You can even feel the singer gaining confidence as the piano supports—but never overwhelms—the words of the song.

A spiritual gift does not have to encompass the world or even the entire church. God may assign us a specific task and equip us with outstanding ability to do it. One person always finds the right words for a note of sympathy or encouragement. Another notices newcomers at church and makes them feel especially welcome. Still another keeps Sunday school supplies orderly so teachers can find what they need. Are these enormous gifts? Yes, to the people who receive the benefit!

REFLECT: *What gifts do you have that you've been dismissing as "too small"? How might they serve the church?*

SANDY LARSEN

Each of you should look not only to your own interests,
but also to the interests of others.

PHILIPPIANS 2 : 4

In our everyone-for-yourself world it's easy to overlook the interests of others. We even think, *If I look out for another's interests, who will look out for mine?* But that doesn't seem to be Paul's concern in Philippians 2:4. The other person is what's important to Paul.

When I was in college (long before the days of the personal computer) I offered my typing skills to those in my hall. I didn't do it to earn money; I simply did it to show love. It often meant late nights for me, but looking out for the interests of others not only benefited them, it also built trust, opening up doors for many conversations about the Lord over the next couple of years.

REFLECT: *What are you good at that may serve others in need? What would it take for you to commit some of your time and energy toward that service?*

CAROLYN CARNEY

Gotta Pray

> *He said to them, "Come with me by yourselves
> to a quiet place and get some rest."*
>
> MARK 6:31

In the Gospel accounts we see that many people responded badly to Jesus, but he weathered those responses without injury. He clearly wanted people to receive him and his Word, but his feelings weren't hurt if they didn't. The primary issue for Jesus is not his own good, but ours. He hopes to hear us pray, not because he needs the affirmation of being asked but because in prayer we are offered an opportunity to build faith. Jesus is not diminished by our absence, but we are.

Learning to spend time alone with Jesus can be a tricky discipline in a wildly overstimulated world. Sometimes it's all we can do to throw ourselves into prayer uttering something like, "Aack!" or perhaps, on a really articulate day, "Help!" But we need to remember that while our time with God is lovely for him, it is absolutely essential for us. And we don't have to worry about doing it right, because Jesus translates all languages—even "Aack!"

A C T : *Identify one fifteen-minute interval each day when you can stop to pray and read the Bible.*

ALISON SIEWERT

Hide and Seek

"Hurry and come down;
for I must stay at your house today."

LUKE 19:5 NRSV

I've often wondered how I would really feel if Jesus showed up at my door. I mean, would I really feel excited? Jesus is an intense guy, and he is, well, God.

What is it like to have God show up at your door? What if he showed up at a bad time—still in your bathrobe, pre-shower, unabated morning breath? Do you imagine yourself running to greet him? Or would you hide in the house till you could get your act together?

Zacchaeus found out when Jesus invited himself over for dinner. Imagine Zac's shock: he had climbed a tree in hopes of simply seeing Jesus from a safe distance, and now the rabbi was coming to his home.

Jesus is interested in us at our worst. In fact, it's only when we encounter him at our worst that we grow into our best.

REFLECT: *What's your first reaction when Jesus shows up?*

ALISON SIEWERT

M O N D A Y *The Recreation Room*

> *"I have told you this so that my joy may be in you*
> *and that your joy may be complete."*

JOHN 15:11

I was on my way out for a night on the town. Jesus stopped me and said, "I would like to go with you."

"Oh," I replied rather awkwardly. "I don't think, Lord, that you would really enjoy where we are going. Let's go out together tomorrow night. Tomorrow night we can go to a Bible class or a social at the church, but tonight I have another engagement."

That evening I felt rotten! What kind of a friend was I to Jesus?

When I returned that evening, I acknowledged, "Lord, I know now I can't have a good time if you are not along. From now on we will do everything together!"

Then we went down together into the rec room of the house. He transformed it. He brought new friendships, new excitement, new joys. Laughter and music have been ringing in the house ever since. With a twinkle in his eye, he smiled, "You thought that with me around you wouldn't have much fun, didn't you?"

REFLECT: *When was the last time you invited Jesus to join you in some fun? When was the last time you deliberately left him behind?*

ROBERT BOYD MUNGER

Holy Play

"You must deny yourselves and not do any work."

LEVITICUS 16:29

A friend of mine who is passionate about roller coasters invited me to go to the amusement park with her. Glad to accompany her but worried about a day away from work and family, I found my fanny pack and went, with guilt, for a play day.

As we walked across the parking lot, she said, "This is great! I am so relaxed." My spirit jolted within me. Relaxed? Was relaxing even possible in an upright position? I don't play well or easily. But I decided to give relaxing and moving at the same time a try and let God take care of my workload.

As the park closed, my voice was hoarse from talking incessantly and screaming on rides, my hair was dripping from a water ride and my heart was surprisingly light. I smiled all the way home, and when I hugged my kids, I said, "Guess what I rode today? You won't believe it!" To my husband, Rich, I said, "What a great day! I'm so relaxed!" And I think I heard God laugh right along with Rich.

A C T : *Holy play creates a holy day. When can you schedule one?*

JANE RUBIETTA

Whale Watching

> *The earth is full of your creatures.*
> *There is the sea, vast and spacious, teeming with creatures beyond number . . .*
> *and the leviathan, which you formed to frolic there.*

P S A L M   1 0 4 : 2 4 - 2 6

Toward the end of every winter, southern right whales begin their migration from Antarctica and head for the shores of Argentina, South Africa and Australia. Thousands of people flock to the shores to watch these delightful creatures hurl themselves out of the water and gracefully lob their tails back and forth. They raise their barnacled heads just above the surface and stealthily move forward, as if they know they are being watched.

Was God beside himself with delight the first time he witnessed one of these sixteen-meter, hundred-ton dancers flail themselves out of the water? Might he have clapped his hands and gasped with amusement? Or perhaps he sat back and said, "Well done."

Why would God create such a creature with such unique habits? Was it for his delight or ours, or simply just because he could? It is ours to ponder this side of heaven. Certainly though, the acrobatic habits of the southern right whale cause me to ponder the grand creativity of the Maker himself.

A C T : *Take a walk and observe the imprint of God's fingers on what he's created in nature.*

CAROLYN CARNEY

Hugging God

I love you, O LORD, my strength.

PSALM 18:1

David's first words, his shout before Psalm 18 begins, are words of love for God. Actually, the Hebrew word David uses is not the normal, vanilla word for love. His word means a yearning love, a burning love, a love that embraces. David wants to wrap his arms around God and hold on!

How long has it been since you felt that much in love with Jesus, so moved with gratitude and adoration that you wished you could put your arms around him and hug him? The next time your heart is moved in deep love for the Lord, do what David did. He spoke words that expressed the feelings of his heart: "I love you, O LORD." And then, who knows, maybe David reached out and up and took the Lord in his embrace.

REFLECT: *When was the last time you were overwhelmed with love for the Lord? Recall the experience of embracing God.*

DOUGLAS CONNELLY

FRIDAY *Laughter and Meetings*

> *Every day they continued to meet together in the temple courts.*
> *They broke bread in their homes and ate together with glad and sincere hearts.*

ACTS 2:46

Rich and I were in a new church and feeling overworked and stressed. Filled with a sense of duty, we headed to an evening meeting that was being held at a church member's home. There, the tenor of the night surprised us. Amidst the business at hand, there was much camaraderie and fun. The evening sped by and we finally looked at our watches, reluctant to leave but needing to trade ministry hats for parenting ones.

We looked at one another, smiling en route to the parsonage, and I asked, "What felt different there?" Together we said, "Oh, the laughter." Being with these people felt like a spa for the spirit. We returned home relaxed and light.

Laughter and meetings, friendship and work don't seem to partner together often enough. But the companionship transformed our night's agenda into a soothing balm. I think it must have felt like that to be with the disciples, crowding around Jesus.

PRAY: *Ask God to lighten your heart, to show you his laughter in the seriousness of your day.*

JANE RUBIETTA

Stop for the Sunset

You have set your glory above the heavens.

PSALM 8:1

With dinner its usual last-minute memory, I hurriedly washed, chopped and sautéed veggies for stir-fry. Josh, twelve, rushed off to visit some neighbors while I cooked and awaited the rest of the family's arrival. The phone rang. My friend Jenni said, "Jane, quick, can I kidnap you?"

"Like, right now, or sometime this week?"

"Now. I'm a few blocks away. I think there's going to be an awesome sunset and I wanted to watch God's glory with you."

Dinner. Family. Pressures. Deadlines. *Forget it,* I thought. Turning off the burner, I said, "Let's do it!"

We drove toward a field and parked along a tiny country road, where we witnessed God's drama intensifying with the shifting of clouds and light. Fifteen short minutes was all it took for me to be filled with God's glory in the presence of a friend. So dinner was a bit late. I think my face glowed, like Moses', from catching the sun's curtain call.

ACT: *What can you do for fun for fifteen minutes? Who can you invite into that adventure?*

JANE RUBIETTA

M O N D A Y   *The Bedroom*

For God is not a God of disorder but of peace.

1   C O R I N T H I A N S   1 4 : 3 3

I halted at our bedroom door, discouraged. Seasonal clothes that wouldn't cram into drawers lay in heaps. Since we were overhauling the bathroom, wood trim, the fixtures and other homeless debris had found their way here. Under the dressing table crouched a TV we didn't want in the children's rooms. The almost-installed kitchen faucet and water purifier graced another area. Dust cloaked every surface.

I had always wanted to reserve the bedroom, of all the places in my home, as a sanctuary for our marriage. I wanted to hang carpenters' helmets and parenting badges and other roles outside the room. But somehow those boundaries had gotten erased. It was no surprise that our marriage didn't feel as close as it once had, that our times of connecting well and deeply occurred less frequently. Marriage appeared to be an afterthought, based on the state of our bedroom.

So yesterday, with the sun's blessing, I prayed for our marriage and started shoveling. It will be nice to welcome my husband home from his trip with a clean room.

REFLECT: *How does your bedroom reflect your deepest longings or your pace of life?*

JANE RUBIETTA

The Bed Is Too Short

"This is the resting place, let the weary rest";
and "This is the place of repose"—but they would not listen.

ISAIAH 28:12

When a friend came to visit me, I gave her my bed while I curled up on my small, hard couch. I was unable to fully stretch out and endured a fitful night. I can't say I wasn't warned about short beds. When the Israelites refused to enter God's rest, they created their own pointless rules and lived hurried lives. God compared such fitful living to poor sleeping conditions. "The bed is too short to stretch out on, the blanket too narrow to wrap around you" (Isaiah 28:20). I too battle the temptation to live fitfully. But a full schedule often makes for an empty soul. Only when I take time to intentionally stretch out and repose my hurried heart do I move from a cramped and cold religion to a full and restful life.

P R A Y : *Lord, teach me to relax, to release stress, to return control to you. Revive my weary soul.*

MARSHA CROCKETT

Rest First

> *It is in vain that you rise up early and go late to rest,*
> *eating the bread of anxious toil; for he gives to his beloved sleep.*

PSALM 127:2 RSV

Hebrew scholars tell us that the Jewish day began at sundown. The creation story says that when God made the world "there was evening, and there was morning—the first day" (Genesis 1:5). In God's mind, then, the day begins with the evening, with rest. In the twenty-first century, we have lost the rhythm of rest first, work second.

Psalm 127:2 reminds us that God gives to us when we are asleep. Sleep is a reminder that we are not in control. It is evidence that our value is not only in our work. God values the fruit of the Spirit in our lives more than our productivity, and sleep is a message of grace. God does not want us to eat "the bread of anxious toil." God invites us to rest in grace.

REFLECT: *As you crawl into bed tonight, remember that you are beginning your day. While you are asleep, God will be at work, in you and around the world.*

ALICE FRYLING

Putting My Soul to Bed

"Father, into your hands I commit my spirit."

LUKE 23:46

Each night before we fall asleep we should prepare our souls to meet God. We should tuck away the cares and concerns of the day and, like Christ, relinquish the failures and successes, the frustrations and delights of each day into God's hands. I have noticed that when I put my soul to bed each night (in contrast to watching movies, reading secular books or just flopping down exhausted) my rest is more tranquil.

Learn the practice of putting your soul to bed with God. Try using a nighttime prayer such as this one from *The Book of Common Prayer*:

Watch, O Lord, with those who wake, or watch, or weep tonight, and give Your angels and saints charge over those who sleep. Tend Your sick ones, O Lord Christ. Rest Your weary ones. Bless Your dying ones. Soothe Your suffering ones. Shield Your joyous ones, and all for Your love's sake. Amen.

ACT: *Put your soul to bed with God, starting tonight.*

KAREN MAINS

F R I D A Y

Sweet Dreams

> *At this I awoke and looked around.*
> *My sleep had been pleasant to me.*
>
> JEREMIAH 31:26

Jeremiah apparently slept well despite spending many of his waking hours deeply traumatized. The weeping prophet could not weep while he was asleep. This troubled man could not worry while he was unconscious. He may even have learned to sleep briefly in the stocks or to catch forty winks in the pit. For a brief period he was totally vulnerable, utterly oblivious and perfectly safe. For he had learned, "He who watches over you will not slumber; indeed, he who watches over Israel will neither slumber nor sleep" (Psalm 121:3-4). Jeremiah woke up pleasantly refreshed, ready to look around and see what the day would bring forth.

With Christ in my heart, I too can sleep safely in God's care, being strengthened by his grace, unconsciously preparing to meet another day.

REFLECT: *For a third of your life you're unconscious. How can you spend it sweetly trusting?*

STUART BRISCOE

Asleep on His Chest

"Come to me, all you who are weary and burdened,
and I will give you rest."

MATTHEW 11:28

One entry in my journal reads as follows:

Very tired. Told God I'd like to just sleep for a few days. Imagined myself sleeping on his chest. Pictured Rich stretched out on the floor, with one of our cranky tired babies lying on top of him, Rich's arms wrapped around the baby. Eventually the baby relaxed and slept soundly. Rich awake, watching with love and a fierce protection, breathing the baby's breath and feeling the tiny heart pound against his chest. I like that image and find myself feeling less tired thinking of it. Thank you, Father, for letting me stretch out emotionally and spiritually on your chest even though physically I need to be awake.

JOURNAL: *Measure your fatigue level. Did you awaken tired? How can your rest be enhanced by feeling the presence of God as you sleep?*

JANE RUBIETTA

MONDAY *The Hall Closet*

You were taught, with regard to your former way of life,
to put off your old self, which is being corrupted by its deceitful desires.

EPHESIANS 4:22

After spending a decade pursuing "deceitful desires," I realized I was the one who was truly deceived, for nothing brings more pleasure than knowing Jesus. Opening my heart to Christ was the first step, the most important step—but hardly the last step. Putting aside my "old self" for good meant facing those things I'd simply put aside for years.

I had taken one sin in particular and tucked it away for safekeeping, like a child clings to a tattered old blanket to comfort him. Many people might not even call it "sin"—only "weakness" or "habit." But I knew it for what it was.

When Jesus brought this sin to my attention, I realized I could not empty that dark closet out myself. And I knew that Jesus could, and would. Indeed he did. For he is the lover of my soul and the cleaning service of my heart.

PRAY: *Lord Jesus, I give you the key to my closet door knowing the contents can no longer hurt me when they're gone.*

LIZ CURTIS HIGGS

TUESDAY *Be Perfect, Therefore*

"Whoever is dishonest with very little will also be dishonest with much."

LUKE 16:10

I was raised to believe that while all sins are offensive to God, there is a hierarchy of greater and lesser sins, each with an appropriate consequence. Therefore, as a child I persuaded myself that "not all that bad" was the same as "acceptable."

Later in life, Luke 16:10 hit me right where I lived: I had to give up, once and for all, this self-serving delusion that "little sins" are not really sinful. But how could I ever give up *all* my indulgences? How could I be perfect, as our heavenly Father is perfect (Matthew 5:48)?

I resisted even trying, knowing I would fail, until I realized that perfection is an ideal, not a commandment. And that was when, with God's love and forgiveness to guide me, I began the painful and never-ending process of cleaning out that cluttered closet.

REFLECT: *How does discouragement affect your pursuit of holiness? Ask God to strengthen your ability to fight sin without becoming paralyzed by failure.*

DAN KLINE

WEDNESDAY

The God Who Recycles

He who was seated on the throne said,
"I am making everything new!"

REVELATION 21:5

Every Wednesday morning, I take trash cans and recycling bins out to the curb. I feel like I'm purging my home of all its impurities, and I come away feeling cleansed.

There's a lot of garbage in our lives. I'm grateful that God will take away my trash if only I am willing to bring it to him. He forgives my sins, no questions asked, and the trash is taken away as far as the east is from the west.

But I'm even more excited about the recycling. It's somehow thrilling to think about cans, bottles, cereal boxes and newspapers being remade and finding new use. God is the Great Recycler. There are times when I feel used up and worn out. I feel useless, like I'm good for nothing. But God can renew me and restore me and use me for service in surprising ways.

PRAY: *Spend some time in confession the next time you take out the garbage. And when you take out the recycling, give thanks for the opportunity to begin again.*

AL HSU

THURSDAY *Increased Enough*

THURSDAY   *Increased Enough*

> *"Little by little I will drive [the Canaanites] out before you,*
> *until you have increased enough to take possession of the land."*

EXODUS 23:30

Exodus 23:28-30 focused a beam of God's light into my heart during one of the most discouraging times in my life as a Christian. I felt defeated and fraudulent. I was lost, confused and full of self-doubt. I felt like I was losing ground in my journey with Jesus.

This passage, read afresh in my heart by the very voice of God's Spirit, told me differently. I had actually come to this recognition of sin because I was finally mature enough to deal with it. At this time, I had "increased enough" to possess the promise on the other side. I began to look at this opportunity for repentance in a new way. Little by little God was making me right, driving out sin. Recognizing the need for repentance was not a sign of losing ground, but of maturing faith.

REFLECT: *How can repentance in your life become an occasion for joy?*

ROBBIE CASTLEMAN

God the Gardener

> *"My Father . . . cuts off every branch in me that bears no fruit,*
> *while every branch that does bear fruit he prunes*
> *so that it will be even more fruitful."*

JOHN 15:1-2

I watched a man pruning a small vineyard not long ago. At first, what he was doing looked cruel. He was cutting away all the dead wood and even slicing back into the living wood. His vineyard looked like a platoon of bleeding stumps. When I asked him why he cut the branches back so far, he said, "If I don't, I get a lot of leaves on these vines but very little fruit." Without regular, rigorous pruning, the vine becomes worthless.

I thought about the man's words when I read John 15. God the Father brings the pruning knife into our lives not to harm us but to make us more productive. He cuts and removes—and it hurts! But the result is more fruit, more Christlikeness.

JOURNAL: *Think of a painful or difficult experience you have been through. In what ways did God use that experience to make you more like Jesus?*

DOUGLAS CONNELLY

Thanks for the Electricity

How wide and long and high and deep is the love of Christ!

EPHESIANS 3:18

Gee, Dad, thanks for the electricity." That's my brother's tongue-in-cheek response when his daughters show favoritism toward their stay-at-home mother. My nieces are too young to know that their father is devoting his energy to providing for their needs. You can understand why, I suppose: every morning he drives off, and they don't see him for eight or nine hours. Then he comes home, usually with no gifts in hand for them. Meanwhile, their mother has taught them to read, colored with them, changed their diapers, fed them and done any number of additional things to show tactile love to them. Dad's contribution is like electricity—for the most part, pretty subtle.

It is entirely appropriate to be grateful for the tangible things we receive from our Maker. He shows his love for us in ways that we recognize, but we have plenty of needs we are unaware of. We get by from day to day because our God loves us beyond our ability to understand.

REFLECT: *Try to grasp the intangible love being shown you today by the people in your life, and thank them for it. Then do the same for God.*

DAVID A. ZIMMERMAN

MONDAY *The Family Room*

"I will give you rest."

MATTHEW 11:28

When my daughters were young, we had a daily ritual after school. They dropped their backpacks near my feet and I looked through the contents, marveling at their successes, talking through their problems. Most days were filled with "Guess what . . ." or "You know what happened . . ." But other days they carried home emotional burdens heavier than any backpack. "Nobody likes me . . ." "My friend didn't wait to walk home with me . . ." And through tears and shaky sighs, they turned over their burdens, knowing that I love them.

But some days, my own heavy heart made it difficult for me to pick up their load too. So I called out the name of the one who bore the weight of the world through his death on the cross. He invites me to pass my load to him, the only one who can claim, "The burden stops here."

JOURNAL: *List the items you are currently lugging around in the backpack of your life. Let Jesus unpack the load and give you rest.*

MARSHA CROCKETT

Whose Team?

"Do you think I came to bring peace on earth?
No, I tell you, but division.
From now on there will be five in one family divided against each other."

LUKE 12:51-52

In the office where I had a temporary job, the management announced a sales contest. Everyone would choose to be on one of two teams, the Vikings or the Packers. On the first day of the contest, employees were to come dressed in either purple and gold or green and gold to represent their chosen team. I didn't (still don't) follow football, so on the given day I wore green, gold and purple. I was immediately called a waffle.

Like a team, a family belongs together, and each member wants to play a part in reaching the family's goals. But what happens when God calls for our loyalty and not all our family members want to join his team? There will be conflict. Jesus tells us to expect it.

PRAY: *Express to God your desire that all of your family will join the Lord's team with you.*

SANDY LARSEN

Out of Deep Waters

He reached down from on high and took hold of me;
he drew me out of deep waters.

PSALM 18:16

Moving into my time with God, my heart felt like a medicine ball because of family struggles. My inability to help one of our children through a rough patch kept me humble, though sometimes numb. This day, I opened to Psalm 18 and began to pray the passage and weep. But when I inserted our child's name into the verses, a miraculous change came over my soul. My worries did not separate me from God but rather took me to him. Plus, personalizing the Scripture in this way brought life to the passage, and my soul felt God's power and passion for my child.

I can pray the psalms for my loved ones, knowing that it is in God's will. And then I can stand aside and see God "draw them out of deep waters."

REFLECT: *Where do you feel helpless with a loved one? What family member is God inviting you to pray for through Scripture?*

JANE RUBIETTA

The sun rose above [Jacob] as he passed Peniel,
and he was limping because of his hip.

GENESIS 32:31

After the death of my second parent I sought out rest in the mountains. I was depleted emotionally and physically. It was late winter, still cold and gray in the mountains, with only occasional signs of spring. I went for a walk, and along the way I was surprised by hope.

A large, dead tree lay spread across a stream. Long having lost its bark, it now lay covered with a green velvety blanket of moss. Nature had reaped a harvest among the dead. The tree looked wise, as if lessons had been learned, as if something were born of her suffering. Amongst the death of winter, here was this hint of life, this vibrant green in a forest of gray.

When does suffering subside and hope begin? How does one live fully after loss? Perhaps like Jacob, we limp. Perhaps we carry on into the next phase of life, not bitter about what was not, but marked by and reminded of the hopeful promise of what is.

JOURNAL: *Where have you found hope when it seemed impossible?*

CAROLYN CARNEY

Peace in the Midst of Ruins

Christ is all, and is in all.

COLOSSIANS 3:11

One early morning, just before I left for work, I passed through the family room and felt as though the life was sucked from my lungs when I witnessed on my television a plane striking the top of the World Trade Center and minutes later another one hitting its twin tower. I don't remember any words, just my hand pressed over my heart as if to stop the bleeding. I was deeply aware of my own breathing, of working hard to keep it controlled. And I prayed through my tears.

In the family room real life and death, both within my own family and within the family of humanity, enter my home. I feel a heightened sense of unity and disunity all at once on days like that day. But I'm also mindful that at both ends of the extremes I find Christ, for he is all and is in all, and in him all things hold together. And the paradox of peace and hope smolder in the ruins of humanity.

JOURNAL: *Describe how hope or peace come to you in the midst of turmoil.*

MARSHA CROCKETT

Anticipating Grace

Mary treasured up all these things and pondered them in her heart.

LUKE 2:19

I had spent days weighing a decision: moving from New York City to Atlanta. But one early May morning, I sat at my desk thinking not of my future but of my mother. I was writing a Mother's Day card. I included a short poem I had recently read, "The Avowal" by Denise Levertov. The poet vows, like a hawk resting on air, to "learn to attain / freefall, and float / into Creator Spirit's deep embrace." As I copied it out, I realized that God was speaking to me—quietly, unexpectedly—and nudging me to risk the move, to trust his grace.

Like the new mother Mary, I soaked up these God-sent words. I moved to Atlanta with them secreted in my heart. I too wondered how my life would change. What would God do? How would he provide? Where would all this lead? At the time, I could not know. I could only anticipate grace.

REFLECT: *What unexpected words or unsettling experiences have come to you lately? Is God speaking? Ponder them in anticipation of his grace.*

BOBBY GROSS

MONDAY *The Back Porch*

> *God's invisible qualities—his eternal power and divine nature—*
> *have been clearly seen, being understood from what has been made.*

ROMANS 1:20

I cherish having a yard, a little green space amid the noise of life. As I sit on our back porch, early in the morning or late at night, I am acutely aware of the goodness and majesty of God, who gives life to every plant and cares about every bird. His majesty winks at me from the night sky. His glory whispers to me in the gentle breezes through the pines and sycamores. His presence surrounds me in the myriad of creatures, great and small, who inhabit the green space in our backyard. Lying in the hammock, I am overcome with joy, and I praise and thank him in whom we live and move and have our being.

ACT: *Take a walk, and consider the glory of God in the creation around you today.*

T. M. MOORE

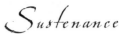

Whatever you do, do it all for the glory of God.

1 C O R I N T H I A N S 1 0 : 3 1

At dinnertime I am usually multitasking. Zooming into the kitchen, phone in hand, I cook and make phone calls. Josh crouches over homework at the table, a leaf caught in the vortex of a whirling eddy of wind. My neck aches from my shoulder-crunch phone hold, the ink on my papers blotches, and Josh disappears emotionally from the commotion. Dinner is late and all conversations fractured by my contaminating stress levels. For years, this pre-dinner chaos reigned.

Today, en route to my desk, I remembered dinner; I had a speaking engagement, but staggered crews of family and guests needed sustenance. Though my work list was long, the thought of providing a hot bowl of stew with fresh bread to nourish my family filled me with joy. Alone, I prayed and prepared, loving the ones who would pull up chairs at various points of the evening. One task at a time is teaching me the ministry of presence, of hospitality with my own family.

R E F L E C T : *What part of the day is most likely to be fractured? How can you work around the craziness with the gift of presence?*

JANE RUBIETTA

"If you consider me a believer in the Lord," she said,
"come and stay at my house."

ACTS 16:15

What do we use a home for? Naturally, it's a place of shelter for our family, and it's where we store all our stuff. But is there more to home ownership than this?

One thing I've learned is that having a house is an opportunity to practice hospitality. Christians are called to welcome the stranger and to befriend the marginalized, so our homes can be places where we build friendships and foster community.

In the same way, if my heart is to be Christ's home, then Jesus would encourage me to think of my life as a place that is welcoming and open to others. Friendship is an act of hospitality in which we welcome others into our lives just as we would host guests in our homes.

If you have given your house over to Jesus, then let it be a place of refuge and ministry to the hurting and searching. And let your life be open to someone today.

ACT: *Practice hospitality by inviting someone over for a meal or to spend an evening visiting with you.*

AL HSU

To him who is able to do immeasurably more than all we ask or imagine . . .
be glory . . . for ever and ever!

EPHESIANS 3:20-21

The girls had made a path across the backyard out of lawn chairs, wagons, slides, boards and an ice chest. They then proceeded to step from one piece to the other as they made their way across the yard. Curious, I asked, "What are you doing?"

"Mommy, stay there. Don't come any further," they warned.

"Why?"

"Because of the hot lava." I nodded my head in understanding. Anyone with half an imagination could see hot lava flowing all over my backyard.

What if, rather than hot lava, my backyard represented my life without Jesus, and the stepping stones were the path he laid out for my safe passage through life? Or, what if the ground was covered by blessings, but I chose to avoid it by perching myself upon my fears and stubbornness? Just imagine. I'd miss being consumed by his love. I need to grasp the unimaginable reality of Christ in me and to let that truth consume me right here and now.

REFLECT: *Imagine what it will be like to meet God face to face.*

MARSHA CROCKETT

A Prayer for Those Not in Need

*May the Lord make your love increase and overflow for each other
and for everyone else, just as ours does for you.*

1 THESSALONIANS 3:12

We know how to pray for people who are sick or out of work. But what about people who are doing well? Most of us don't even pray for those who are not in need.

Paul was proud of the Thessalonian church. The Christians in that city were submissive to God and enthusiastic in their witness. They were doing it right! But Paul didn't scratch them off his prayer list. In fact, he probably prayed even more for them.

One of the things Paul asked God to do in this prospering church was to make their love increase. They were already a loving group, but Paul prayed for more. Did you ever pray that God would make a loving Christian even more loving, or that a wise Christian would abound in wisdom? Praying for people *not* in need just might transform your prayer life.

PRAY: *Think of some Christian friends who are doing well. Ask God to strengthen areas in their lives that are already strong.*

DOUGLAS CONNELLY

> *Always be prepared to give . . . the reason for the hope that you have.*
> *But do this with gentleness and respect.*

1 PETER 3:15

I lose every debate in my family. I give up before it starts.

My brother and my sister each took debate classes in high school; I did not, and I swear that to this day they could convince me, if they wanted, that night is day and I owe them money.

The thing about debate classes is that you wind up arguing for whatever is assigned to you, regardless of what you believe. As such, you learn to turn your passion on and off. You can debate someone—your brother, for example— wholeheartedly one moment and give him a hug the next.

There's a lesson there for the rest of us, and even our faith is subject to this lesson. We are to defend the faith with passion, but we are to do it with gentleness and respect. After all, our debate partners are our brothers and sisters, and we love them, don't we?

ACT: *Read a book that teaches you how to defend Christianity against its critics. Then read a book about loving your neighbor.*

DAVID A. ZIMMERMAN

MONDAY *The Attic*

> *"Come, let us return to the LORD.*
> *He has torn us to pieces but he will heal us."*

HOSEA 6:1

For a period of years I doubted God's goodness. His actions in people's lives and in the world seemed random. Then a phone call from a good friend surprised me. We had lost touch and not seen each other for seven years. She happened to be in the neighborhood and wanted to see me.

I'd had no idea what she'd been through during those seven years. It was a remarkable tale of her marriage nearly breaking up, infidelity, a terrible accident, separation, walking away from God, involvement in a cult—but in the end, God mended the brokenness. At the end of her story, Mandy exclaimed, "God has been so good."

Even in my coldness of heart, I could not deny that God had woven together the broken pieces of Mandy's life to create a beautiful tapestry that reflected his faithfulness. Sometimes seeing God's goodness to another can melt our own blaming and unforgiving hearts.

REFLECT: *As you look back on difficult times in your life, how do you now see the hand of God?*

CAROLYN CARNEY

TUESDAY *Dispensing Comfort*

The God of all comfort . . . comforts us in all our troubles,
so that we can comfort those in any trouble
with the comfort we ourselves have received from God.

2 CORINTHIANS 1:3-4

God allows trouble to come into our lives so that we will learn how to comfort others. Who can better understand the loss of a mate than someone who has lost a mate? Who can better share the pain of divorce or the agony of a child's death or the frustration of prolonged unemployment than someone who has been through that pain and who has experienced the comfort of God in that pain?

In that sense, *no* suffering is ever a dead end. God's promise always gives some purpose to the difficulties we endure. If you have experienced some of life's wounds and are hiding them, you are wasting valuable education. The body of Christ desperately needs people who are willing to show their scars.

ACT: *If you are facing a trial, seek out other believers to help you. If you are not facing a trial, offer your help to someone who is.*

DOUGLAS CONNELLY

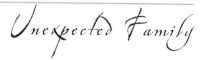
Unexpected Family

My purpose is that they may be encouraged in heart and united in love.

COLOSSIANS 2 : 2

A new friend called me this morning. Her husband pastors the church my husband, Rich, attended as a small child, and a couple of years ago Rich helped with worship there. He connected well with their family, encouraging their daughter as she pondered a possible engagement. Her mother phoned me this summer, asking if I'd lead a women's retreat, and miraculously before she called God had directed me to all the material I'd need to prepare for the topic she wanted.

Now the daughter, married and ready to deliver twins, was in danger, and her mother had called two weeks ago to ask me to pray—a remarkable privilege considering we'd never met in person. We prayed on the phone, and this morning she called to say the babies had been born by C-section. I hung up rejoicing in God's goodness and creativity at weaving our lives together, beginning forty years ago in a tiny church. You never know when family will turn up.

A C T : *Recall a friend from your past. Whatever happened to them? See if you can find out.*

JANE RUBIETTA

We will tell the next generation the praiseworthy deeds of the LORD,
his power, and the wonders he has done.

PSALM 78:4

M any of my Sunday school students are unfamiliar with the Bible. They've heard some stories about Moses and Noah and Jesus, but that's the extent of their knowledge. I love how they react to something they've never read before. Their eyes get enormous. They look at me, then back at the Bible and then back at me. They say, "*Really?*" "Jesus did *what?*" That's much more fun than "Ho hum, I've heard it all before."

You don't have to teach Sunday school to "tell the next generation the praiseworthy deeds of the LORD." If you know a young person who is struggling with some timeless human problem, you can point that person to a Scripture passage that has helped you. You can relate a time when you realized God's love in a fresh way or received some insight about his character. You can tell how God rescued you, whether physically or spiritually or both. The stories of God are never outdated.

REFLECT: *Think of a young person who needs encouragement. What Scripture or personal story can you pass along to him or her?*

SANDY LARSEN

The Comfort of Friends

A friend loves at all times, and a brother is born for adversity.

PROVERBS 17:17

Johnny was supposed to be home from school at a certain time each day. One day he was particularly late. When he came in his mother asked, "Where have you been?"

"I had to help a friend."

"Well, what happened?" asked his mother.

"My friend fell down and started to cry."

"And what did you do?"

"I sat down and cried with him."

Real friends comfort by letting us know that we are not alone in our human frailties. I cannot begin to tell you the number of times I have been strengthened because someone came alongside of me to comfort me. Sometimes it was simply someone saying to me, "I'm praying for you." At other times it was someone taking me out to lunch and cheering me on. Our family has been blessed by the generosity of special people who have provided frequent-flier miles or a condo on the beach so we could get away for rest and restoration. In what practical ways can you extend comfort to your friends today?

A C T : *Make a list of people who would benefit from specific acts of kindness from you. Schedule each act of kindness into the coming weeks.*

RICK EZELL

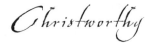 *Christworthy*

> *Whoever loves father or mother, . . . son or daughter more than me is not worthy of me;*
> *and whoever does not take up the cross and follow me is not worthy of me.*

MATTHEW 10:37-38 NRSV

What do you love most in life? Your family? Your friends? Your work? Your art? What do you most fear? Rejection? Loss? Failure? Suffering? Death? Jesus expects his disciples to love him above all else and to follow him despite our fears.

As an enthusiastic teenage Christian, I wore a cross and carried a Bible to school. My society-conscious grandmother acidly chided me and pressed her daughter to forbid my embarrassing display. Mom refused. My grandmother didn't speak to either of us for six months. I shrugged it off, but it stung my mother, testing her allegiance to Christ.

Ridicule costs something; parental rejection costs more; physical persecution costs the most. Is Jesus worth it? Each September on Holy Cross Day we recall that Jesus gave up the things he loved and endured the cross he feared—for us. Are we worthy of him?

REFLECT: *Are the expectations of someone keeping you from doing anything Christ expects?*

BOBBY GROSS

MONDAY *Transferring the Title*

Search me, O God, and know my heart;
test me and know my anxious thoughts.

PSALM 139:23

Opening a clean journal on January 1, I glanced back at the previous year's collection. Worried entries about finances glared at me, yet when I looked at God's provisions, all the worry seemed wasteful of time and faith. "This year," I promised a friend, "I am not worrying every day over money. I'm watching for God to show up and trusting more that he will."

Finances are one of the final bastions for me in turning my worries over to God. Was he capable of providing for two self-employed "missionaries"? Yes. Had he seemed willing to provide? Yes. So what was the problem?

So often I didn't know in advance where the money would come from. But faith—believing in what is not seen—depends on history, not on knowing the future, right? And three years' worth of journals documented God's history with us.

My journals display God's faithfulness. Maybe the title transfer isn't total yet, but increasingly, God holds the key.

REFLECT: *What is your last bastion in transferring the title to God? What holds you back?*

JANE RUBIETTA

T U E S D A Y *Desperate for God*

> *She came up behind him in the crowd and touched his cloak,*
> *because she thought, "If I just touch his clothes, I will be healed."*

MARK 5:27-28

The woman with the hemorrhage in Mark 5:24-34 was as desperate as they come. Her illness meant she was cut off from her community, a topic of conversation but probably not anyone's dinner guest. She was an oddity, and a pitiful one at that. Her illness made her weak, and she lived daily with the shame brought on by her "unclean" status.

Touch is part of daily life: a handshake, a touch on the shoulder, a kiss on the cheek. Imagine if every time people went to shake your hand, they'd either think twice about it or immediately wash their hands and go to the synagogue for ceremonial cleansing. Imagine the shame you would feel, the isolation.

This woman had reached the point of hopelessness. There was only one choice left to her, and so in her desperation, she reached out for Jesus.

JOURNAL: *Recall a time you felt desperate as you reached out for Jesus. What did he do for you?*

CAROLYN CARNEY

Thirst Quencher

"I am thirsty."

JOHN 19:28

A few years ago a commercial suggested that when we get that hungry feeling at about 4:00 p.m., we should reach for a Snickers candy bar, because "Snickers really satisfies." However, what your body is craving at 4:00 p.m. is probably not a candy bar but a glass of water. Dehydration is often misread as hunger.

I am not always aware of my true thirst. Cheap imitations satisfy me momentarily but inevitably leave my soul in want. I am like the Samaritan woman trudging every day to the well to temporarily quench my thirst, when all along Jesus is offering himself to slake my thirst in all ways and for all time.

REFLECT: *Are you misinterpreting your soul's thirst as some ambiguous hunger? Ask Jesus to satisfy your thirst.*

CAROLYN CARNEY

Losing It More Each Day

"Whoever wants to save his life will lose it,
but whoever loses his life for me will find it."

MATTHEW 16:25

When, in the summer of 1973, I turned the deed of my life over to Jesus Christ, many people thought, "Colson's lost it." They might have more accurately said, "Colson's losing it." I have been losing my life for Jesus Christ increasingly with each passing year, and I'm discovering that the more of Chuck Colson I set aside, the more of Jesus I'm able to enjoy.

Throughout my life I was always passionate about whatever I did, whether as a lieutenant in the Marines, in law, in politics as an aide to a U.S. senator or serving as an assistant to the President. But the passion I felt for those endeavors pales into insignificance compared to the passion I feel for Jesus. With Jesus holding the note on my life, I live in the freedom and joy of seeing him work in me, and this is the greatest reward any man or woman could possibly have.

REFLECT: *What have you lost as you've turned over more of your life to Jesus? What have you gained?*

CHARLES W. COLSON

FRIDAY

Safe at Home

> *Fear of man will prove to be a snare,*
> *but whoever trusts in the LORD is kept safe.*

PROVERBS 29:25

Both my husband and I travel a lot, sometimes together, but often in two separate directions. At night, especially when I am alone, I dutifully lock the door and set the house alarm.

It's not just us. People, organizations and governments have all become increasingly mindful of security. It makes sense to be as careful as possible. But in the end, what does security mean? Double bolting our doors and windows? Heeding the warnings of the Department of Homeland Security? Storing away cases of bottled water and rolls of duct tape and a transistor radio with extra batteries in a place where we can easily grab them?

Maybe, but then again, maybe not. Real security comes from knowing we have put our trust in the Lord God.

REFLECT: *In what have you put your trust? What are you doing to demonstrate this?*

KAY MARSHALL STROM

Time

> *Now is the time of God's favor,*
> *now is the day of salvation.*

2 C O R I N T H I A N S 6 : 2

When my daughter was an infant I worked away from the home and worried that I wasn't spending enough time with her. When she turned two, I quit my job to stay at home full-time. My grief was replaced with the shocking realization that the time we now spent together had become mundane, filled with routine chores and little money for "fun."

Then I read a thought by Pablo Casals that has sweetened the minutes of my life: "Each second we live in a new and unique moment of the universe, a moment that never was before and never will be again."

Christ indwelling my heart and my home makes life worth living. It's okay to dream and plan for the future. It's fine to reminisce about the past. But the time I hold in my hand right now is all I will ever possess. And with each new minute, Jesus creates a sacred opportunity to make the most of this moment in time.

A C T : *Take the next thirty minutes to be fully present and aware of what you see and hear, touch and taste.*

MARSHA CROCKETT

Fall

MONDAY

Making Your Heart a Home

"If a man loves me, he will keep my word, and my Father will love him,
and we will come to him and make our home with him."

JOHN 14:23

Jesus told his disciples that though he would be leaving to prepare a place for them, they could at the same time prepare a place for him in their hearts. He would come and make his home with them right here.

This was beyond their comprehension. How could it be?

Then came Pentecost. The Spirit was given to the church, and now they understood. God did not dwell in Herod's Temple in Jerusalem—nor in any temple made with hands! Now, through the miracle of the outpoured Spirit, God would dwell in human hearts.

Thirty minutes after Pentecost the disciples knew more about Jesus than they had known in the three years previously. It is difficult for me to think of a higher privilege than to make for Christ a home in my heart, to welcome, to serve, to please and to know him there.

REFLECT: *Imagine a relationship with Jesus without the indwelling presence of the Holy Spirit. Thank God for the gift of knowing him intimately.*

ROBERT BOYD MUNGER

The Secret to Life

> *"Store up for yourselves treasures in heaven. . . .*
> *For where your treasure is, there your heart will be also."*

MATTHEW 6:20-21

Nothing in my home is more than thirteen years old. Not my furniture or my dishes or anything in my clothes closet. Not even anything in my garage or attic. I don't own anything old.

I used to. But our family home burned to the ground thirteen years ago. A lifetime of treasures reduced to a pile of ashes.

Today, as I look at our collection of new things, I wonder which ones I could live without. The answer is: every single one of them! My things have plenty of value to me, but as my family learned from the insurance company, value is all a matter of perspective.

My pastor once said, "Here is the secret to life: Learn to love the right things." The only things worth loving—*really* loving—are those that have eternal value.

JOURNAL: *What are the most important things in your life? How much of your time, energy and resources are you putting into them?*

KAY MARSHALL STROM

WEDNESDAY *A Simple Request*

"Could you not keep watch for one hour?"

MARK 14:37

Jesus made a simple request: "Sit here. Watch. And pray." Peter, James and John were not asked to perform miracles, preach to crowds of people or give away all they owned. All they had to do was sit, watch and pray. But a little while later, they were all asleep.

Peter had boasted a few hours earlier that he would, if necessary, die for Christ. The others all said the same thing. But Jesus hadn't asked them to die for him. All he had asked of them was one hour of watching and praying.

Jesus isn't looking for people with lofty intentions. He isn't concerned about our great speeches of what we will do for him. Jesus is looking for people who will follow his simple instructions.

REFLECT: *What is Jesus asking you to do today?*

DOUGLAS CONNELLY

> *"Listen! I am standing at the door, knocking; if you hear my voice and open the door,*
> *I will come in to you and eat with you, and you with me."*

REVELATION 3:20 NRSV

Imagine that a buyer falls in love with your house and contracts to purchase it. During the month before settlement, you remove several walls, convert the living room into a kitchen and board up windows in the bedrooms. Finally, you have the house moved to a different lot. On settlement day, the buyer receives a vastly different home than anticipated.

How often we get caught up trying to modify our lives in ways Christ doesn't desire in our effort to conform to some "ideal Christian personality." In contrast, Jesus offers a simple promise: hear his voice and open the door, and he'll come in to us. He has given us our individuality for a purpose. God endows us from birth with a unique "inmost being" (Psalm 139:13). The life we commit to him is a *distinctive* life.

As the purchaser of any home would do, Jesus will "remodel" our lives in important ways. But his concern is with changing our character, not our personalities. It is with our individual gifts that we are able to serve him uniquely.

P R A Y : *Thank God for how he has gifted you. Pray for greater understanding of how you might use your gifts.*

M. BLAINE SMITH

FRIDAY

The LORD confides in those who fear him.

PSALM 25:14

When I make God my Lord, he confides his secret thoughts to me. He shares what's on his heart with me through his Spirit. Some days he calls me to weep with him over the brokenness and pain of the world. Some days he invites me to encourage his other children. Some days he whispers tender words to me, and I'm swept away by his amazing grace.

But as much as he longs to confide in me, I must first prepare my heart and mind each day to receive him, to bow before him and exalt him in my life. And so I come and lay down my distractions, presenting my disappointments and concerns not just to empty my basket full of heartache but to make room for his presence. And when I do, he tells me "Fear not . . . Don't worry . . . Cast all your cares on me." And with such tenderness I enter the glory of intimate union with the Holy One, my Confidant.

PRAY: *Ask God to give you his view of events, circumstances and individuals, and enter into prayer in union with his heart.*

MARSHA CROCKETT

Gone Fishing

"Come, follow me," Jesus said, "and I will make you fishers of men."
At once they left their nets and followed him.

MATTHEW 4:19-20

Fishing was good business in Galilee. The lake provided a prosperous life for Peter and Andrew and James and John. They had spent a lot of time with Jesus over the past months; now the challenge came to travel with him full-time. His call was simple: "Follow me." Immediately the men left their nets and boats and followed. It wasn't easy to leave fishing; it was their livelihood, their life, all they had ever known. But Jesus' invitation was irresistible. They would no longer be fishing for food for the table; they would be fishing for citizens for the kingdom.

PRAY: *Ask God to help you to focus your heart more on his interests than your own.*

DOUGLAS CONNELLY

M O N D A Y

The Study

> *Within your temple, O God, we meditate on your unfailing love.*
>
> PSALM 48:9

My study is a small room with thick walls. But in a sense, it is the control room of the house.

When Jesus entered this room with me and looked around at the books in the bookcase, the magazines on the table, the pictures on the walls, I became uncomfortable. There were books his eyes were too pure to look at, and magazines a Christian has no business reading. As for the pictures—the imaginations and thoughts of my mind—some of these were shameful.

I turned to him and said, "Master, I know this room really needs to be cleaned up and made over. Will you help me change it to the way it ought to be?"

He gave me a full-sized portrait of himself. "Hang this centrally," he said, "on the wall of the mind." I did, and I have discovered through the years that when my thoughts are centered on Christ, the awareness of his presence, purity and power causes wrong and impure thoughts to back away. So, though the struggle remains, he has helped me to bring my thoughts under his control.

REFLECT: *What place does the Word of God and the presence of Jesus have in your mind? What can you do to center your mind more consistently on Christ?*

ROBERT BOYD MUNGER

The Fruit of Study

> *Do your best to present yourself to God as one approved,*
> *a workman who does not need to be ashamed*
> *and who correctly handles the word of truth.*

2 TIMOTHY 2:15

Jonathan Edwards had the discipline—and the luxury—to spend fourteen hours a day in his study.

My study looks more like a landfill than a library. Yet it is in my study, seeking the Lord in prayer, reflecting on his Word, poring over the thoughts of my contemporaries and forebears in the faith or preparing some teaching or writing assignment, where many of my most significant encounters with Christ have occurred.

The Lord never lets me rest on my accumulated knowledge but always draws me on to deeper truths, fresher insights and more visionary undertakings in his name. Study is not vain; it helps to bring forth the fruit of righteousness in every area of my life.

A C T : *Select one book of Scripture to study in depth over the coming weeks. Ask your pastor to recommend some resources for learning the background of your chosen book.*

T. M. MOORE

W E D N E S D A Y

Self-Emptying Obedience

Your attitude should be the same as that of Christ Jesus:
who . . . made himself nothing.

PHILIPPIANS 2:5-7

In the New Testament, nearly 30 percent of the Greek words for "think" are used in the four-chaptered letter to the Philippians. Why? Because its author, the apostle Paul, was not where he wanted to be. Paul was in jail. He resorted to *thinking* through his faith when *feeling* faithful was hard.

Paul's greatest gifts were sidelined by his imprisonment. But in Jesus he saw the self-emptying life of obedience in each moment as the answer to his dilemma. So, when Paul couldn't be "out there" making disciples, he wrote a letter to a church he loved. He emptied himself in that moment and is still discipling the church two thousand years later.

R E F L E C T : *What do you wish were different about your life? How can you follow Christ through your current circumstances?*

ROBBIE CASTLEMAN

Come Quickly!

> *"I will shake all nations . . . and I will fill this house with glory,"*
> *says the LORD Almighty.*
>
> HAGGAI 2:7

Reading the morning newspaper can be a practice in frustration. From all around the world come endless reports of trouble and corruption of those in power. Oppression and injustice, it seems, are everywhere. "Where is God?" we ask. "Why doesn't he *do* something?"

Good news! He will. Haggai prophesies of a time when God will grab up all the powerful rulers in the world and shake out every bit of their precious treasures. All the piles of gold and silver that tumble forth from them will be nothing compared to God's great glory.

If you are discouraged about the hopelessness of world affairs, don't despair. Put down the newspaper and take up God's Word.

PRAY: *Using the newspaper as a guide, pray for the troubles revealed there, that God will show his glory through the course of events.*

KAY MARSHALL STROM

Until we all reach unity in the faith and in the knowledge of the Son of God
and become mature, attaining to the whole measure of the fullness of Christ.

EPHESIANS 4:13

Spiritual maturity is having a life that resembles Christ's. Age, knowledge, activity and zeal would be easier standards by far. But God's standard, his meaning of *maturity*, is none of these things. The only measurement that counts, according to Ephesians 4:13, is how much we are like Jesus.

On a wall near the main entrance to the Alamo in San Antonio, Texas, is a portrait with the following inscription: "James Butler Bonham—no picture of him exists. This portrait is of his nephew, Major James Bonham, deceased, who greatly resembled his uncle. It is placed here by his family that people may know the appearance of the man who died for freedom."

No portrait of Jesus exists either. But his likeness is to be seen in us, his followers, as we grow to maturity.

REFLECT: *Who would people say you remind them of? What would need to change in you for them to say, "Jesus"?*

RICK EZELL

No Secrets, No Fears

What we are is plain to God.

2 CORINTHIANS 5:11

The apostle Paul carried out his work in the world with nothing hidden. His enemies said that he was just trying to build an empire for himself. They accused him of trying to milk people for money. But Paul's answer to every accusation was this: "I am ready right now to stand before Christ."

I wonder what you and I would have to get rid of before the Lord could search our desks or our Internet files. I wonder what we would have to repay or what relationships we would have to reconcile if we knew that at five o'clock tomorrow we would give an account to God.

Paul kept close watch on his life. He lived each day in the conviction that everything about him was totally open to God. He was ready to be displayed. No secrets, no fears.

REFLECT: *How closely do you live to Paul's openness? What can you do today to move yourself closer to a transparent life?*

DOUGLAS CONNELLY

MONDAY

The Dining Room

"Get up and eat, for the journey is too much for you."

1 KINGS 19:7

In transition (and perhaps in smooth waters as well), our physical appetites become monitors for our spiritual health. When my husband and I felt God leading us into a new ministry and financially precarious territory, I alternately clung to God and, panic-stricken, did everything I could to trim expenses. Nearly every waking moment reminded me of our uncertain future. Anxiety gnawed a hole in my heart. Sometimes I noticed hunger, but I mostly ignored the sensation, returning to work and worry.

When a friend came for a coffee run, I folded my long body into her tiny car. She eyed me kindly, saying, "We wish you would eat more, Jane." I was stunned. Returning home, I weighed myself. Down fifteen pounds. How had that happened?

Our appetites will teach us, if we listen, where and on what we are feeding. Does my neglect of food at critical times indicate my level of trust in God? Is the same thing true when I indulge in anxiety eating?

JOURNAL: *What do your eating habits say about the condition of your soul?*

JANE RUBIETTA

Teach Me to Wait

Be completely humble and gentle;
be patient, bearing with one another in love.

EPHESIANS 4:2

I always feel convicted when I read the account in Genesis 27 of Rebekah conspiring to trick her blind husband, Isaac, into giving Esau's birthright to Jacob. I'd like to think I would never do such a thing, but I have to admit, I get awfully impatient waiting for God's timing.

Patience just doesn't seem to be a natural human trait. But instant gratification is not God's way. Consider this:

- It took centuries for the Savior to come into the world.
- It took him thirty years to start his ministry.
- It took three days for him to rise from the dead.
- For two thousand years, Christ's followers have been awaiting his return.

When I get impatient with God's timing, I think about Rebekah. Her way didn't work out well at all. Jacob was forced to run for his life, and as far as we know, Rebekah never saw her beloved son again. Today my prayer is this: "Teach me, dear Lord, to be patient. Teach me to wait on your timing."

REFLECT: *In what situation do you need to practice waiting on the Lord?*

KAY MARSHALL STROM

Anxiety Prayed to Rest

Do not be anxious about anything,
but in everything, by prayer and petition,
with thanksgiving, present your requests to God.

PHILIPPIANS 4:6

Do not be anxious about anything . . ." Right! It's obvious that Paul didn't live in the twenty-first century, when terrorists could strike anywhere at any time. Where our kids aren't safe and we dare not leave our homes unlocked. Where there is more persecution of Christians than ever before, and . . .

But wait a minute. Paul lived in the first century when the Romans were in the process of overrunning the known world. When the life expectancy was only around thirty-five. When Christians were being martyred in horrible ways. Oh, yes, and he was in prison when he wrote this verse.

If anyone had a reason to be anxious, it was Paul. Yet he wrote that we are to focus on gladness, to be gentle with others, to pray with a thankful heart. "And the peace of God, which transcends all understanding, will guard your hearts and your minds in Christ Jesus" (Philippians 4:7).

JOURNAL: *What aspects of life cause you the most anxiety? What prevents you from presenting those anxieties irrevocably to God?*

KAY MARSHALL STROM

THURSDAY   *The Right Place*

> *One evening David got up from his bed*
> *and walked around on the roof of the palace.*
> *From the roof he saw a woman bathing. . . .*
> *David sent messengers to get her . . . and he slept with her.*

2 SAMUEL 11:2, 4

David was king of Israel, a person of faith and character. But one night he became careless. He was in the wrong place *physically*. He should have been leading his men on the battlefront. Instead, he relaxed at the palace. He was in the wrong place *relationally*. He was alone, lacking the emotional support he needed to keep his hormones in check. He was in the wrong place *mentally*. He allowed his mind to wander. He was thinking impure thoughts. He was in the wrong place *spiritually*. He glossed over his disobedience. He covered it up, thinking that if no human knew about it, God wouldn't know about it either.

Lust reaps its greatest havoc on our lives when we are in a tempting place, when our minds are not guarded and when we are spiritually distant from God.

REFLECT: *Where are you most vulnerable to temptation—physically, relationally, mentally or spiritually? How can you guard yourself in that area?*

RICK EZELL

Give Thanks

> *Whatever you do . . . do it all in the name of the Lord Jesus,*
> *giving thanks to God the Father through him.*

COLOSSIANS 3:17

Thanks for the good supper!" How pleasing it is for me to hear my children say such words of unsolicited appreciation. Expressing gratitude does not come easier to adults than it does to children. We usually think most about what we want rather than about how much we have.

One of our basic sins is not saying thanks to God (see Romans 1:21). God regards our thankfulness so highly that he calls it a sacrifice (see Psalm 116:17). How can saying thanks to him be a sacrifice? It's a sacrifice to take our minds off ourselves and think about God, to consider his gifts and goodness rather than our own problems.

God says that one proof of our love for him is our gratitude. If we care enough, we will take time to say thank you to God. Our words and our actions will show that we do not take him for granted.

P R A Y : *Take a moment to consider all that you have, and express your appreciation to God.*

JAMES REAPSOME

St. Michael and All Angels

> *And there was war in heaven.*
> *Michael and his angels fought against the dragon.*
>
> REVELATION 12:7

I once belonged to an Episcopal church called All Angels', and each year we remembered and gave thanks for the mysterious ministry of angels. In recent popular culture, angels have seemed ubiquitous. Many think of them in the same vein as leprechauns or unicorns.

But in the Bible, angels are truly ubiquitous and fearfully real. They act as *warriors*, as in the captain who confronted Joshua or the surrounding army Elisha was given to see. They serve as *messengers*, as in Gabriel, who spoke to Mary, or the pair at Jesus' tomb. They appear as *guardians*, as in the one who shut lion jaws for Daniel or unlocked prison gates for Peter.

We would do well to remember, not once a year but daily, that we live our lives amidst a contest between light and darkness, good and evil, and that powerful beings fight for us and guard us. Let us remember Michael and all angels.

P R A Y : *Give thanks today for the (usually) unseen ministry of angels—and take heart!*

BOBBY GROSS

M O N D A Y

The Living Room

> *"Be still, and know that I am God; I will be exalted in the nations,*
> *I will be exalted in the earth."*

P S A L M   4 6 : 1 0

I awaken to the sun streaming through the window, and worries rush in like saltwater on the *Titanic*. How to pay the bills? Handle difficult parenting issues? Meet this deadline, that need?

I force myself to breathe steadily and say to God, "I give up." This prayer is becoming more a part of my life these days. I give up my attempts to control the universe, to manipulate the outcome of a meeting. I give up my anger at someone, my unforgiveness of another. I give up my fear for a friend, for the future, for the schedule. I give up my weakness and inabilities. I just give up, and I breathe some more.

And when I give up, God comes near. He scrapes the load together and hauls it off, smiling as though I've given him a present. Maybe I have. I've given him my heart, once again. And he's exchanged it for peace.

R E F L E C T : *Consider the hardest things to give up. Can you list them and relinquish them to Christ now?*

JANE RUBIETTA

Statement of Faith

*Always be prepared to give an answer to everyone who asks you
to give the reason for the hope that you have.*

1 PETER 3:15

Challenged to write out my own personal statement of faith one evening, I penned these words to God:

> I believe you are the Creator and Sustainer of all things, living and inanimate, spiritual and physical, intellectual and emotional. For this reason I believe that in you, for you, and through you I find purpose, ability and reason to live and move and have my being. Without your breath of life, I would crumble into billions of dust particles. And by your breath of life I am revived, complete and held together. . . . I believe you are the great I AM, eternally present, without constraint of time, limitless in power and beauty, mercy and love, justice and holiness. Your glory, beyond brilliance, radiates throughout the universe. . . . You alone are worthy of praise. Let my life blaze with praises to you, Almighty God, Great Jehovah, Abba Father. Amen.

JOURNAL: *Draft a statement of faith beginning with the words "I believe."*

MARSHA CROCKETT

God of the Storm

> *The voice of the LORD is over the waters;*
> *the God of glory thunders, the LORD thunders over the mighty waters.*

PSALM 29:3

I love thunderstorms! I get up at night when the thunder starts rumbling, and I watch the lightning flash and the wind blow.

I'm in good company watching thunderstorms; the psalmist and king, David, liked them too. On the occasion in Psalm 29:3 he watched a big one move in from the sea. He heard more in the storm than booms and crashes. He heard the Lord—not in words, but in a dramatic demonstration of his power. David's heart leapt in adoration of God.

The God who can control a powerful storm can also protect his people. Think about that the next time you find yourself in a storm. Don't hide under the covers. Watch for a while, and let your heart praise the God who sits enthroned above it.

PRAY: *Give me ears to hear your voice and eyes to see your glory, Lord—even in a storm.*

DOUGLAS CONNELLY

No Thanks

One of them, when he saw he was healed, came back,
praising God in a loud voice.

LUKE 17:15

Several years ago a mentor and friend challenged me to cultivate a new habit. He suggested that I take time each day for gratitude—not the "thank-you-Lord-for-all-your-goodness" gratitude, but appreciation for specific gifts and blessings that God had provided.

My friend took me back to the incident in Jesus' life when he healed ten men afflicted with leprosy. "Go, show yourselves to the priests," Jesus said, and as they obeyed Jesus' command, they were healed (see Luke 17:14). Only one man, however, returned to thank Jesus. "Where are the other nine?" he asked (Luke 17:17).

Ten were healed, but only one expressed his gratitude. The other nine were so excited about their healing they forgot the Healer. I've done the same thing, and so have you. We are so caught up in the blessings that we forget to thank the Blesser. Jesus told the man who returned, "Your faith has made you well" (Luke 17:19). Ten men were healed; one man's life was changed forever.

PRAY: *Make a list of specific people, things or events you have benefited from in the past twenty-four hours. Thank God for each.*

DOUGLAS CONNELLY

Fortress of Solitude

Now when Jesus saw great crowds around him,
he gave orders to go over to the other side.

MATTHEW 8:18 NRSV

Superman flies all the way from Metropolis to the North Pole when he needs some time alone. I'm surprised he ever comes back, actually. All he gets from Metropolis is one cataclysm after another.

The North Pole, cold and distant, is one way to get some time to yourself; it screams "Keep out!" to virtually everyone who might otherwise interrupt you. But solitude has a higher purpose than mere seclusion. A discipline among Christians from the beginning, taking time away from everyday sights and sounds allows more space and time to hear what desperately needs hearing: God's word to us and our own subconscious cry to God. Once such intimate conversation takes place, we can return to the task God has called us to. After all, Jesus took time away regularly, but he always came back when the time was right.

Metropolis would be a cataclysmic place if Superman never left the North Pole. But Superman ought never settle for the chaos that life in Metropolis would relentlessly hurl at him. He is, after all, only human.

ACT: *Open your calendar and schedule a day of solitude. Pray that God would grant you the courage to keep the appointment.*

DAVID A. ZIMMERMAN

Zero Degrees of Separation

> *"He is not far from each one of us.*
> *'For in him we live and move and have our being.'"*

ACTS 17:27-28

I am never far from the hand of God. Neither are you.

Beyond the metaphysical weirdness of that statement—I'm in Chicago, for all I know you may be on the international space station, and yet God is with both of us—such a statement can elicit radically different emotions.

When I'm insecure, I might react to the thought of an ever-present God with resentment. *Can't I just have a day to myself? What does God want from me now?* In moments like this God's presence may seem suffocating. We may not necessarily even be doing anything wrong; we just wish we had a little space.

But can God really help being there for us? He is, after all, looking after us, as any parent ought. And it's not likely that, left to our own devices, we would survive the harshness of one another, not to mention the creation that turned against us as a result of our sin. Think about it long enough, and you'll be forever grateful that God is always present, never sleeping.

JOURNAL: *Recall a time you felt suffocated by God. Why did God stick with you when you wanted him to go away?*

DAVID A. ZIMMERMAN

M O N D A Y
The Workroom

> *The midwives, however, feared God*
> *and did not do what the king of Egypt had told them to do;*
> *they let the boys live.*
>
> EXODUS 1:17

Sometimes being obedient to God and doing the right thing is hard. It can even get us into big trouble with employers, friends or family. At the beginning of Exodus, Pharaoh was afraid of the strength and numbers of the tribes of Israel living in Egypt, so he enslaved them and commanded the midwives to kill all the baby boys. But Shiphrah and Puah, the Hebrew midwives, refused to do this great evil. They took a huge risk in disobeying Pharaoh, because they knew that their higher authority was God. Scripture says that because of their obedience, "God was kind to the midwives and the people increased and became even more numerous. And because the midwives feared God, he gave them families of their own" (Exodus 1:20-21). Even before Moses came onto the scene, God used these two faithful women because they were willing to follow him in their day-to-day work no matter what the cost.

REFLECT: *Who in your day needs the strength of your faith and courage?*

STEVE HAYNER

Good Citizenship

Conduct yourselves in a manner worthy of the gospel of Christ.

PHILIPPIANS 1:27

In elementary school, you probably got a grade on your report card for citizenship. That grade covered your behavior, your attitude, your work habits, your conduct on the playground.

Conduct. That's the word Paul uses in Philippians to talk about our Christian behavior. He's rounding up every aspect of our lives—not just our conduct on Sunday in church but also our conduct at home and at work. He includes the choices we make, the words we use and the way we drive. Every aspect of our citizenship is to measure up to the message of the gospel. Our conduct is to support our claim to be a follower of Christ. How we live should equal what we believe. What will your report card say?

JOURNAL: *Grade your conduct: "Plays well (or doesn't play well) with others"; "Shows respect (or lacks respect) for God's authority." Hold a conference with God and brainstorm some ways to improve your grade.*

DOUGLAS CONNELLY

Faithful in Little

> *"Whoever can be trusted with very little can also be trusted with much,*
> *and whoever is dishonest with very little will also be dishonest with much."*

LUKE 16:10

A friend of ours likes to say, "I wish God would give me a chance to show what I could do for him if I was really rich."

I too whine about all that I wish I had—until I measure myself against the majority of people in the world who have so much less. I groan about my physical limitations—until I see the seemingly insurmountable physical challenges some people have overcome in order to serve the Lord. I complain that there just are not enough hours in the day—until I read about the amazing accomplishments of people who only lived to be half my age.

And so I end up on my knees. No, I don't ask for more money, or for greater health, or for a longer life. My prayer is simply this: "Please, Lord, help me to be trustworthy with whatever you give me."

REFLECT: *Is there an area of life in which you need to be more faithful? What can you do to practice that faithfulness?*

KAY MARSHALL STROM

A Meal Interrupted

He got up from the meal, took off his outer clothing,
and wrapped a towel around his waist.

JOHN 13:4

It never fails! The minute we sit down to eat a meal together, the phone rings. Some cosmic law brings our phone number up on every telemarketer's list just after we take our first bite. My response is to say, "Don't answer it." My wife's response is to say, "Maybe someone needs us."

Last night the call came right on schedule. "Don't answer it," I said as Karen picked up the phone. On the other end of the line was a friend in tears who needed to talk. Karen's supper got cold. The rest of us finished eating and had our dishes in the dishwasher before the conversation ended.

When Jesus got up during the meal to wash the disciples' feet, he was showing us that sometimes our investment in the lives of others brings interruptions. Our plans, at times, have to be set aside because of the needs around us.

PRAY: *Help me to go through life, Lord, willing to serve no matter what the circumstances.*

DOUGLAS CONNELLY

Doing the Impossible

Be strong in the Lord and in his mighty power.

EPHESIANS 6:10

When God calls us, not once does he recommend that we fulfill the calling in our own strength; never does he suggest that we are to accomplish his calling with our own cleverness or skill. In fact, Scripture doesn't ever point to our sufficiency but rather points to our weakness, our inabilities. Sometimes it seems that the more impossible the dream, the more likely it is that God is calling us.

That's why I love speaking: I get to see God work miracles in people's hearts, things that I could never make happen on my own. I love being called to the impossible, the unattainable, because then I am certain that the hand of God must come through. My dependency on the power of God has increased a thousand percent as I've trusted him to speak, to write, to love through me. And then, God gets the glory. What a divine, no-fail setup!

JOURNAL: *Where have you seen God's glory and strength when you've been faithful to use your gifts?*

JANE RUBIETTA

Time for Breakfast

When they landed, they saw a fire of burning coals there with fish on it,
and some bread. Jesus said to them,
"Bring some of the fish you have just caught."

J O H N   2 1 : 9 - 1 0

My father was quintessentially Irish: his thoughts rarely made their way into spoken words, but frequently they became his actions. My brothers and I were quite surprised when he named his company MCD Electric (Michael, Carolyn and David). He was not one to verbalize his love, but he let his actions speak.

In John 21:9-10, as the disciples labored, Jesus, who had already given his life for the sins of the world and was appearing to them now as the resurrected Lord, cooked breakfast for his weary followers. This simple image reminds me that my actions are just as important as my words.

Peter had denied Jesus; Thomas had doubted him; many had left Jerusalem altogether for fear of reprisals. But Jesus did not hold any of this against his friends. It was not time for a sermon; it was time for breakfast.

R E F L E C T : *What are some ways you can show your love by serving others today?*

CAROLYN CARNEY

M O N D A Y   *The Recreation Room*

> *We loved you so much that we were delighted to share with you*
> *not only the gospel of God but our lives as well.*
>
> 1 THESSALONIANS 2:8

St. Francis said, "Preach the gospel and when necessary use words."

His words took on special meaning for me with my friend Robin in high school. We'd play sports together or go for coffee, and we'd engage in stimulating discussions of faith that ended with Robin expressing doubts or objections. One evening we made a date to meet, but Robin didn't show up on time. Late into the night, however, she finally arrived, very drunk and very apologetic: "I don't know why you just don't give up on me." God gave me the words to respond, "I won't give up on you because Jesus doesn't give up on you." Sharing my life with Robin was just as important as explaining the gospel story.

REFLECT: *In what ways can your life—your hobbies, interests and even struggles—bless your friends this week?*

CAROLYN CARNEY

*For what is our hope, our joy, or the crown in which we will glory
in the presence of our Lord Jesus when he comes? Is it not you?*

1 THESSALONIANS 2:19

We hadn't heard from Glenn in about twenty-five years when unexpected circumstances put us in touch with him again. Now when we get a letter from him, everything stops until we read it. He writes about his work for the Lord, his family and his travels. Usually he has some funny anecdote, and he almost always mentions some new spiritual insight.

Why are we so interested in hearing from Glenn? Because about thirty years ago when he was a teenager we were privileged to have some part in his spiritual growth. He will always be a joy to us. When you help someone move closer to Christ, even by a small degree, that person enters into your heart's joy and stays there. Whether you remain close or lose touch, your heart will keep a special reserve of joy for that one whom God touched through you.

P R A Y : *Ask God to grant you the joy today of bringing others closer to him.*

SANDY LARSEN

Speak Creatively

> *My heart is stirred by a noble theme as I recite my verses for the king;*
> *my tongue is the pen of a skillful writer.*

PSALM 45:1

God spoke—or perhaps sang!—creation into being. And when God made humans in his image, he gave us the gifts of language and creativity. To speak, especially to speak creatively, is to be human. Indeed, when we describe how the Creator took on humanity, we say, "The Word became flesh" (John 1:14).

I am especially grateful for poets and songwriters and the writers of homilies, those who use language with craft and creativity. They enable us to see and hear and feel extraordinarily. Like the psalmists, they enable us to convey our thoughts, to express our love, to voice our praise with greater power and beauty. And maybe they inspire us to venture into our own creative expressions.

ACT: *Share with someone close to you a piece of art, a song or poem, or a book that has helped you to experience the love of God in fresh ways.*

BOBBY GROSS

The Earth Is the Lord's

The earth is the LORD'S and everything in it.

PSALM 24:1

Who decided that reading was more spiritual than, say, walking through a forest preserve or chasing raindrops with a toddler?

My guess is that it was a monk. For hundreds of years they were the people most likely to be literate. But then again, monks like Francis of Assisi are remembered more for their acts than for their writings, and Francis's *Canticle of the Earth* doesn't celebrate reading—it celebrates, among other things, trees and rain.

Christianity is a literary faith, of course. Known as "people of the book" at different times in our history, most of us have the Word of God available whenever we feel led to read. But there's no commandment in the Bible that says, "Only as thou readest wilt thou incur the blessing of thy God." God gave us his Word, but he gave us this world as well. When we open ourselves to his creation, we open ourselves to our Creator.

ACT: *Sometime this weekend, set aside your devotional. Take your devotions outside and enjoy God's creation.*

DAVID A. ZIMMERMAN

F R I D A Y *Melt My Heart*

Do not put out the Spirit's fire.

1 THESSALONIANS 5:19

During the winter months, I use the fireplace in my living room more days than not. I love a fire partly for the warmth but also for the scent, the sound, the sight and the delight of the atmosphere. On cold mornings my children awaken, head straight for the hearth and pull their knees up under their chins to warm themselves as their bodies and minds meet the day.

I also love the fire because it becomes my prayer in picture form: "Light a fire of passionate love within me, O Lord. Let it melt my cold heart like wax near the flame. Burn away all that does not please you. Use the trash that clutters my mind to kindle the fire and refine my thoughts. Let me bask in the warmth of your presence today."

REFLECT: *Imagine the Spirit of God as fire. Does the image warm your heart? Refine your thoughts? Destroy your sin?*

MARSHA CROCKETT

Laughing Matters

Sarah said, "God has brought me laughter,
and everyone who hears about this will laugh with me."

GENESIS 21:6

You don't hear a lot about Christian comedians. That's strange, because being a Christian gives you plenty to laugh about.

If Christians are anything, we're human, which means we will inevitably find ourselves in laughable situations. Sarah even named her son "Isaac," or "Laughter," remembering that God's promise of a son had initially sounded quite comical to her. We repeat the same sins over and over; we sing lines like "Let it be a sweet, sweet sound to your ear" off-key; we turn beet-red as we debate which worship songs should be sung in our church. It can all be pretty funny when you think about it.

It's entirely possible that many of us will see no serious spiritual breakthroughs in our lives until we learn to laugh at ourselves. And that's funny, in a sad sort of way.

JOURNAL: *What in your Christian life would have less power over you if you could laugh at it? What prevents you from laughing at it?*

DAVID A. ZIMMERMAN

M O N D A Y — *The Bedroom*

"I made a covenant with my eyes not to look lustfully."

JOB 31:1

Almost every man I know has at some point in his life wrestled with pornography. And significant numbers of women are lured into sexual fantasy too. Cable television, video technology and the privacy of the Internet have all brought sexual images into our homes and into our hearts.

Job knew nothing of modern technology, but he had an incredible grasp of how temptation captures us. He made a covenant, a solemn agreement, with his eyes. He made up his mind that he would not give his eyes access to images that would lead his heart astray.

When I was a teenager and wanted to go some place questionable, my mother would ask just one question: Can you take Jesus with you? I thought it was corny then, but that shows how immature I was. Would you be comfortable inviting Jesus to watch the DVD you rented last week? Could he sit with you while you surf the Web? Could you hand the novel you are reading to the Holy Spirit?

ACT: *Print Job 31:1 and tape it above your television screen or computer monitor.*

DOUGLAS CONNELLY

TUESDAY   *God's Standard*

> *It is God's will that you should be sanctified:*
> *that you should avoid sexual immorality.*

1 THESSALONIANS 4:3

When it comes to sexuality, the world says, "It's your body, your right, your future. Do what you want." As a result, people have been hurt and abused, and they live with guilt, disease and unwanted children. God's standard, on the other hand, is not always the easy thing to do, but it is the right thing to do. God created sex to be enjoyed within the boundaries of marriage.

God is not the cosmic killjoy here. He says no to sex outside the marriage bond for our protection. When we abide by his standard, we receive peace, protection, security and intimacy.

REFLECT: *Which cultural messages about sexuality stick with you the most? How can Scripture help you to make sense of those messages?*

RICK EZELL

Drawing the Line

"Blessed are the pure in heart,
for they will see God."

MATTHEW 5:8

One week while I was still dating, God began to speak to my heart: *Pam, you and Bill have made the obedient choice not to have sex before marriage, but just how do you plan on keeping that commitment? How far will you go physically?* The Spirit whispered, *Push the line back to where you can maintain a pure heart toward Bill.*

At the end of our next date, Bill asked for a kiss, and I said, "Bill, I really, really want to say yes, but God is telling me that I need to say no. So, no."

We maintained that boundary until he proposed, and we maintained our virginity until our wedding night. I believe that is why we have a vibrant sex life now, nearly twenty-five years later.

PRAY: *Ask God for continual help in pursuing purity in your sexuality.*

PAM FARREL

When Love Reverses

> *Then Amnon hated her with intense hatred.*
> *In fact, he hated her more than he had loved her.*

2 SAMUEL 13:15

For months we watched as our neighbor and her sometimes live-in boyfriend fought and were reconciled and fought again. One day Diane said to me bluntly, "You think Todd and I should be married, don't you?" It was not a simple question. Yes, if a couple are going to live together then they should be married. But for Todd and Diane the best thing would have been for them to separate.

Love does not flourish in the poisoned ground of sexual sin, as we see in the story of Amnon and Tamar in 2 Samuel 13. To the shock of both partners, hatred soon springs up instead. God has prescribed that sexual relations should be kept safely within the bounds of loving and committed marriage. If sex is kept there, the weeds of hate will never have a chance to choke out love.

REFLECT: *Where is the Lord nudging your conscience about sexual purity? Confess and forsake any sin in this area.*

SANDY LARSEN

Fulfilling Sexual Desires

> *Since there is so much immorality, each man should have his own wife,*
> *and each woman her own husband.*

1 CORINTHIANS 7:2

Sexual desire is God-given and, in its proper place, healthy and good. In conjunction with other reasons, such as love and the desire for companionship, the desire for sexual fulfillment is a strong and natural motivation for marriage. Love that produces the desire in a man and a woman to commit to a lifelong relationship also generates the desire to express that love sexually. But by itself, the desire for sex is a poor and shallow reason for getting married.

Believers who are serious about their commitment to Christ will seek to fulfill their sexual needs and desires in a godly way. Marriage is the God-ordained vehicle for fulfilling God-given sexual desire.

REFLECT: *How can you be certain that your desires are in line with God's standards?*

MYLES MUNROE

The Purity Principle

The evil deeds of a wicked man ensnare him;
the cords of his sin hold him fast.
He will die for lack of discipline, led astray by his own great folly.

PROVERBS 5:22-23

A believer recovering from sexual addiction once told me, "Addicts always think they can get away with it. You won't change until you realize you can't."

Purity is always smart; impurity is always stupid. Proverbs depicts the man seduced into adultery as "like an ox going to the slaughter" (Proverbs 7:22). The adulterer will be ensnared; he will die. He's the primary victim of his foolishness. In contrast, the man who remains pure can "rejoice" and "be captivated" by his wife's love and enjoy their sexual relationship (see Proverbs 5:18-19).

I can never get away with sexual immorality. God wants me to remember that, not only for his sake and my family's, but for my sake.

REFLECT: *What practical steps can you take this week to guard yourself from impurity?*

RANDY ALCORN

M O N D A Y

The Hall Closet

> *"But store up for yourselves treasures in heaven. . . .*
> *For where your treasure is, there you heart will be also."*

MATTHEW 6:20-21

I love the simple beauty Anne Morrow Lindbergh discovered in the bare beach house where she wrote the classic book *Gifts from the Sea*:

> One collects material possessions not only for security, comfort or vanity, but for beauty as well. Is your seashell house not ugly and bare? No, it is beautiful my house. It is base, of course, but the wind, the sun, the smell of pines blow through its bareness. The unfinished beams of the roof are veiled by cobwebs. They are lovely, I think, gazing up at them with new eyes; they soften the hard lines of the rafters as gray hairs soften the lines on a middle-aged face.

I've decided that a simple life keeps my spirit free from the unneeded "stuff" that binds me to the world. It's time to let go of the possessions hidden in dark closets and to uncover the eternal light of a life hidden in Christ.

REFLECT: *What material possessions are of great value to you? Consider how you can give them over to the lordship of Christ.*

MARSHA CROCKETT

Repentance

> *"Repent, then, and turn to God, so that your sins may be wiped out,*
> *that times of refreshing may come from the Lord."*

ACTS 3:19

*R*epent! We easily stereotype this as the fiery rebuke of revivalists calling for dramatic, once-and-for-all turnarounds from doomed sinners. Well, okay. But sometimes "Repent!" is more like an invitation. Weave the pattern of repentance—looking at yourself, admitting your wrongs and choosing to change—into your life's fabric, and you will be blessed. Whenever I practice this rhythm before God, my sins, which weary me like a sinus infection, are wiped out. I sense God's cleansing presence. I am spiritually refreshed.

PRAY: *Do you need a fresh experience of God's cleansing presence? If so, then respond to Peter's invitation in Acts 3 today.*

BOBBY GROSS

Amazing Grace

You, O Lord, are a compassionate and gracious God.

PSALM 86:15

God is a God of grace. It is at the heart of his nature. It springs spontaneously from his love for us. It is his unexplained joy at giving something priceless to the totally impoverished. It is, according to the Scriptures, unconditional, unlimited, unending, unmerited, unearned and undeserved. Grace does not begin with the sinner's need but with God's desire. It is the norm of Christianity. To miss God's grace is to miss him.

We, the recipients of God's grace, are like commoners who have been touched by the king. We aren't good enough to be chosen, but we have been given a chance. We are living a life we don't deserve and didn't earn—all on the basis of God's amazing grace.

REFLECT: *In what ways has God given you another chance? Offer your thanks.*

RICK EZELL

We take captive every thought to make it obedient to Christ.

2 CORINTHIANS 10:5

We live in the communication age, in which we are constantly assaulted by the television, the Internet, billboards and magazines. We are lured into thinking that happiness is found in having lots of toys, a beautiful body and freedom to do whatever we want, whenever we want. And it's all pumped right into our own homes, if we allow it.

What about filling our imaginations with the stuff of heaven? Every behavior, every passion begins with a thought, a seed planted in our minds. To stay passionately in pursuit of God requires that we feed our minds with the right stuff. To stay enamored with Christ, we must bathe our minds with a vision of eternity and with the dazzling beauty of Christ.

REFLECT: *With what do you fill your thoughts? What can you do today to feed your mind with the things of God?*

ANDY PARK

F R I D A Y

Decay Brings Growth

You have taken off your old self . . . and have put on the new self.

COLOSSIANS 3 : 9 - 10

Turning leaves bring both beauty and sadness. We love the brilliant colors, but we dislike the thought of winter's onslaught. Nature covers decay with beauty, but without decay future growth would be impossible.

In some ways our lives resemble the trees. We have to shed certain things if new life is to come. What the apostle Paul calls "putting to death" we might call "allowing to decay." We must put to death, or allow to decay, things like fornication, indecency, lust, foul cravings, ruthless greed, anger, passion, malice, cursing and filthy talk (see Colossians 3:5-8). Unless these things fall like so many leaves, there will be no room for new behaviors: things like compassion, kindness, humility, gentleness, patience, forbearance, forgiveness and gratitude (see Colossians 3:12-15).

JOURNAL: *Describe a time you mourned the decay of something beautiful only to realize that the loss brought something wonderful and new.*

JAMES REAPSOME

All Saints Day

Therefore, since we are surrounded by such a great cloud of witnesses,
let us throw off everything that hinders. . . . Let us fix our eyes on Jesus.

HEBREWS 12:1-2

When I ran my first marathon, I found myself thinking of the runners—Tiffany, Mike, Brian—who had inspired me to attempt such a thing at the age of forty-seven. I knew they were pulling for me, and I didn't want to let them down. Shortly after finishing the marathon, I phoned each of them, exultant. They whooped with me, sharing my sense of accomplishment and joy.

In the same way, we can draw strength and courage from exemplary spiritual lives, whether we read of them in Scripture, learn of them in history or know of them personally. This is why Hebrews rehearses a roster of "saints," men and women of faith and faithfulness, and then points to Jesus as our ultimate model.

REFLECT: *Think of a saint, living or past. How would that person respond to the responsibilities or situations that you face today? How will you?*

BOBBY GROSS

M O N D A Y *The Family Room*

"Where two or three come together in my name, there am I with them."

MATTHEW 18:20

Healthy family life develops and grows through relationships. These ties are strengthened by times of informal fellowship where news is exchanged on the happenings of the day, where people are able to freely talk about their thoughts and feelings, where decisions of common interests and concern are made, and where one can have some fun. Here we can feel like an important member of the family, loved and cared for by other members.

I have found family oneness in meetings with thousands of strangers around me, or even in a fellowship of believers whose language I did not understand. But I was most vitally joined with others as functioning members of Christ's body in a small group, relating to people as I would to a family of brothers and sisters.

In small groups, we help one another know Christ better and fulfill his purpose for our lives. We can relax, being casual and completely at ease. Even with differences and disagreements, the atmosphere of openness and acceptance in a small group draw people closer to one another—as would happen in any family.

REFLECT: *Who make up the "nuclear family" of your faith? What relationships are helping you to know Christ better and fulfill his purposes?*

ROBERT BOYD MUNGER

Flocking Together

Let us not give up meeting together, as some are in the habit of doing,
but let us encourage one another—and all the more as you see the Day approaching.

HEBREWS 10:25

On this fall day, robins are all over the yard. They're hopping everywhere, pulling up worms, flying up into the dogwood to pluck red berries. A couple of late babies, breasts still spotted, start to poke the ground with their beaks when their parents refuse to feed them. Every move of the birds conveys urgency. It's fall, and their relentless instinct tells them it's time to go.

Some birds migrate singly. Robins migrate in flocks. Perhaps they feel safer together. Or they help each other find food. Or they are warmer when they roost together on cold nights.

Christians are on a long journey of faith. We will do better to make the trip together than to try to fly alone. It is harder to disguise our faults when we flock together, but in each other's company we are more likely to stay safe, nourish ourselves and find comfort.

REFLECT: *Who is on your faith journey with you? Thank God for those people.*

SANDY LARSEN

Family Ties

> *"Who are my mother and my brothers? . . .*
> *Whoever does God's will is my brother and sister and mother."*

MARK 3:33, 35

Some of Jesus' most difficult opposition came from the people who should have been the most supportive of him—his own family. Maybe you know what that is like. You have tried to do the will of God, and the biggest roadblock came from your own parents or brothers and sisters or a spouse.

On this occasion, Jesus' mother and brothers heard about Jesus' exhausting schedule and concluded that he was about to have a breakdown. So (in the dramatic language Mark uses) they came to "arrest" Jesus and force him to relax for a while.

Jesus, however, did not see this as compassion; he saw it as distraction from what God the Father had called him to do. What Jesus makes clear is that when there is a conflict between what God clearly says and the advice or desires of our family, we are to obey God. When opposition came from his human family, Jesus found encouragement in his spiritual family.

A C T : *Express your gratitude to someone who stimulates you to do the will of God.*

DOUGLAS CONNELLY

The Dreaded "S" Word

Submit to one another out of reverence for Christ.

EPHESIANS 5:21

No one likes to submit. It is not in our nature. So when we read the biblical writing about submission, we either think we're supposed to be a doormat or we say that this verse is culturally obsolete. Actually, the word *submit* has military roots and means "to fall in rank under the authority of another . . . to subject oneself for the purpose of obeying or pleasing another." Submission is having the courage to give up my rights to meet another person's needs. It is unselfish behavior that considers the other person first.

While mature, healthy relationships require a balance between giving and receiving, spontaneous unselfishness is the essence of a growing marriage. Real love asks that we put our own needs on hold and respond to our mate's—not endlessly, not unilaterally, but often. In fact, we feel more "in love" when giving to a partner than when receiving.

ACT: *Look for ways you can give up your rights in order to meet the needs of a person close to you.*

RICK EZELL

Spiritual Best Friends

"For where two or three come together in my name, there am I with them."

MATTHEW 18:20

When my husband and I were asked to give our testimonies in church, I knew exactly what Dan would say, and I knew it would bring tears to his eyes. I wasn't certain what I would say, however. My story isn't nearly as dramatic as his. But Dan knew. "You will tell about Micah 6:6-8—the verses that changed your life, won't you?" he said to me. Of course. That's exactly what I would say.

Dan and I have shared a lot of things in the years we have been together, but perhaps the most precious of all has been the sharing of our spiritual selves. We love our how-we-got-here-in-the-Lord stories. We enjoy reading the Bible out loud to each other. We treasure the opportunity to pray together.

Dan and I are more than just dearest friends—we are dearest spiritual friends.

A C T : *Make a list of the spiritual highlights of your life. Make time today to share one of them with the person closest to you.*

KAY MARSHALL STROM

Outward and Upward

> *He and all his family were devout and God-fearing;*
> *he gave generously to those in need and prayed to God regularly.*

ACTS 10:2

When I asked the mother of a busy family whether her daughter would be at youth group the following week, she answered, "We don't even know what's going on tomorrow; we can't plan a week ahead!" She spoke from the frustration of a stressed and overscheduled household.

The obvious solution for hectic family life would be to slow down and put family first. But I've noticed that the strongest families are not those in which family is an end in itself, but those in which all family members work together in the service of something larger than themselves. In one brief sentence the book of Acts shows us the family of the Roman centurion Cornelius. We do not see a scattered, slapdash family life. Here is a family focused on both "outward" and "upward" pursuits. They gave to those in need (outward) and they prayed to God (upward).

REFLECT: *What or whom does your family serve? Talk about changes you can make to focus your family on Christ and others.*

SANDY LARSEN

MONDAY

The Back Porch

> There is neither Jew nor Greek, slave nor free, male nor female,
> for you are all one in Christ Jesus.

GALATIANS 3:28

In South Africa *ubuntu* is a word used to describe a notion of generosity, hospitality and compassion. *Ubuntu* led Nelson Mandela, at his inauguration as president in a country in which he had been a political prisoner for twenty-seven years, to invite two of his prison guards to sit with him on the dais. It is *ubuntu* that led to a peaceful transition in Mandela's government, on a continent notorious for bloody governmental turnovers.

You don't need to look far to find a biblical framework for *ubuntu*. There is the call to Abraham to bless the nations. There are Isaiah's words to care for the marginalized and poor, and there are Jesus' own words: "Love your neighbor as yourself" (Matthew 22:39).

Ubuntu is about valuing others as if they were our brothers and sisters, as if they were our own selves. This is not radical Christianity. It is the gospel. It is what Christ calls us to. Jesus had *ubuntu*.

REFLECT: *How can you fill your actions with unbuntu as a reflection of Christ's love?*

CAROLYN CARNEY

Loving Christ on Earth

*"So in everything, do to others what you would have them do to you,
for this sums up the Law and the Prophets."*

MATTHEW 7:12

Margaret is the ninety-four-year-old mother of my husband Dan's first wife. She is a dear lady who still lives on her own, but she does need help. Most days I don't mind taking her dinner and spending time with her. But now and then I get impatient—or lazy—or I begin to feel that my time is too important to spend talking about the same things we talked about the day before and the day before that.

It's easy to think about serving the Lord and ministering to others in terms of going to faraway places and working with people of different cultures. But just to be faithful to one elderly lady? Why do I have so much trouble remembering that she too is worthy of my love and time and prayerful concern? In the end, her eternity is between her and God. My job is simply to be faithful.

REFLECT: *What can you do today to minister to someone who is in need of your time and attention?*

KAY MARSHALL STROM

He appointed twelve—designating them apostles—
that they might be with him.

MARK 3 : 14

Jesus was a man who needed friends, just like we do. When discouragement or criticism or opposition swallows our dreams, we need a small group of friends who are committed to us.

What strikes me is that Jesus didn't limit his circle of friends just to people like himself. He chose all kinds of men to be his friends. Some were well known; others were unknown. Some talked all the time; some barely said a word. A few of his friends came from the political left; at least one was a radical right-winger.

The point is: don't limit yourself to one kind of friend or to one group of friends. Spread your life out a little. Get to know people older than you and younger than you and poorer than you and different than you. If you want to be like Jesus, cultivate a wide circle of friends.

A C T : *Think of one person who is on the outer fringes of your circle of friends. Take the risk of developing a closer relationship with that person.*

DOUGLAS CONNELLY

Beyond the Status Quo

"You are the light of the world. A city on a hill cannot be hidden."

MATTHEW 5:14

Pulling up to the inner-city church, we looked around. Broken windows. Litter. Iron bars. Security lights. Our church's family mission project sat in front of us, and I had a feeling that our status quo was about to be upset.

Inside, we scrubbed, sanded, painted, laughed and worshiped alongside our African American brothers and sisters. Our school-aged children, Ruthie and Zak, melded instantly with the local kids, and six-month-old Joshua seemed perfectly content in the dark arms of his surrogate nanny. In the closing worship service, members' radiant faces told amazing stories of God's provision in places of poverty, brokenness, relational devastation and peril. "You gotta have a testimony," the preacher said.

I wondered about my own testimony: safe community, safe church, safe life. What was God calling us to do? Within three months, he'd moved us to a near-urban church with high crime and unemployment and raw sewage running down the hill. Our testimony was just beginning.

REFLECT: *Where is God challenging you to move beyond the status quo to make a difference for Jesus' sake?*

JANE RUBIETTA

F R I D A Y

Loving the Unlovely

*"I tell you the truth,
whatever you did for one of the least of these brothers of mine,
you did for me."*

MATTHEW 25:40

My daughter didn't eat Thanksgiving dinner with the rest of the family last year. She was busy helping to serve a meal to the homeless. "But it's Thanksgiving," I said to her when she told me she wouldn't be at her usual place at our table.

"I know," she said. "It is for them too."

It isn't too difficult to help the needy when all we have to do is sit in the comfort of our homes and write a check. But if we are to truly share God's heart, we must look at the world through his eyes. That means reaching out to those in need: the chronically ill, the person who has made bad choices, those who suffer from poverty and injustice.

There is not enough goodness in me to do this. It can only happen when I allow God to use me as his hands and feet here on earth.

REFLECT: *Who in your life is hard to love? How can you show your love for God in your relationship with them?*

KAY MARSHALL STROM

How Big Is Your Life?

Now the Lord said to Abram,
"Go . . . and I will make of you a great nation, . . .
and in you all the families of the earth shall be blessed."

GENESIS 12:1-3

How do we know God? God told Abram that it would be through the people of God, God's own nation made through Abram, that the world would come to know Yahweh. God made it clear this would be a great blessing to Abram and his family, *and* to those who received the knowledge of God through his lineage. Jesus picks up right there in the Gospels, establishing the church as the conduit of God's continued blessing to the world.

How do we live our lives and use our resources? Do we conceive of ourselves as members of such a world-shaping lineage?

REFLECT: *This morning, consider your part in God's saving of the world. Tonight, think back on how God worked through you during the day.*

ALISON SIEWERT

M O N D A Y

The Attic

I thank my God every time I remember you.

PHILIPPIANS 1:3

When I was first paralyzed, I retreated into my memories for comfort and reassurance. In fact, I wasted weeks—even months—dreaming about days when I was on my feet. When depression began to overwhelm me, I realized I had allowed memory to become my enemy. From then on, I decided to treat my remembrances with respect and gratitude. I would *thank God for them,* just as his Word told me to do. They would provide a "journal" of God's faithfulness in my life, and they would serve as hints and omens of even greater things to come in heaven. Memory should be a springboard for catapulting our walk with Christ forward, reinforcing the good things God has done in our past and shoring up our faith for what he will do in the future.

REFLECT: *Delight in your memories, but don't become lost in them. Use happy memories for grateful reflection and to foster hope and confidence.*

JONI EARECKSON TADA

Memorial Stones

These stones are to be a memorial to the people of Israel forever.

JOSHUA 4:7

I walked through the ashes of what had been our house, searching for something I could keep, when I stumbled over something. It looked like a piece of modern sculpture. The base was formed by a set of turkey-shaped salt and pepper shakers, forever melted beak to beak. They had been a gift from my sixth grade teacher who had always expressed such faith in me. On top of them was the melted base of a silver candlestick we got as a wedding gift. To one side was the melted remains of my grandmother's milk-glass pitcher, and on the other a delicate china cup I bought on our honeymoon. Balanced on one end was my daughter's baby spoon and fork, and on the other my son's long-handled baby spoon. The entire piece was glazed over with a sparkling layer of melted crystal.

In our new house, the "memorial stone" sits on a special shelf. Whenever someone asks, "What's that?" I answer, "It's a memorial to God's faithfulness. Our house burned, but our home was preserved."

REFLECT: *What in your history merits a memorial stone?*

KAY MARSHALL STROM

Treasure Up These Things

> *Walk about Zion, go around her, count her towers,*
> *consider well her ramparts, view her citadels,*
> *that you may tell of them to the next generation.*

PSALM 48:12-13

Psalm 48:12-14 has long been a reminder of my legacy of faith that reaches from one generation to the next. It challenges me to walk about the dwelling place of God, to count the ways he empowers me, picks me up, enables me in my weakness. The ramparts are his protection and the citadels his outposts of support and love filled with godly people ready to stand with me throughout my life.

When I think on these things, I ponder the treasure of God's provision for me and my family. "Treasuring up these things," as Scripture says Mary did at the birth of Christ, is an active process of saving memories and recording thoughts. Then, like water tumbling over rough rocks, our ordinary days emerge as polished stones and stand as memorials to God's presence in our families and in our homes.

A C T : *Commit to using journals, scrapbooks, photography or art to reflect God's presence in your life to the next generation.*

MARSHA CROCKETT

Giving Thanks

One of them, when he saw he was healed,
came back, praising God in a loud voice.
He threw himself at Jesus' feet and thanked him.

LUKE 17:15-16

Ten lepers approached Jesus crying for mercy. Jesus responded. He sent them to show themselves to the priests, and as they went, they were healed. But only one, a Samaritan, returned to say thank you.

Why do we so often take our blessings for granted? Do we somehow think we are privileged or deserving or self-reliant or just plain lucky? Do we believe that we have a right to health, happiness and prosperity? Not the grateful Samaritan. He had known prejudice and sickness, pain and loss. Maybe he had known the taste of despair. So on this day, his heart was soft, his feet quick, his praise loud. This was his Thanksgiving Day!

REFLECT: *Today, give thanks to God—and maybe to a few merciful people in your life as well.*

BOBBY GROSS

FRIDAY

"Wash yourselves; make yourselves clean."

ISAIAH 1:16 NRSV

Sometimes a shower is just the thing. After a long day, a difficult conversation, a stack of disappointments, standing under a stream of warm water is precisely what I need to feel cleaned up, refreshed and renewed. The shower can be an easy place to pray too. You're alone and relaxed.

Showers cleanse and reset us. So does Jesus. Old hymns about being "washed in the blood of the Lamb" are accurate descriptions of what Jesus does for us. He possesses the power to clean us up, to give us a new start. And that is precisely what he does.

PRAY: *Ask God to make you aware of what needs to be washed off, and invite him to clean you up.*

ALISON SIEWERT

Fill My Cup

> LORD, *you have assigned me my portion and my cup; . . .*
> *surely I have a delightful inheritance.*

PSALM 16:5-6

When I was a little girl, my mother often delighted my sister and me with surprise tea parties. She had several beautiful teacups and a brilliant green-and-gold porcelain teapot from which she poured the steamy brew. Choosing a cup was always a highlight of our ritual, and we knew we were loved because Mom readily shared her treasured teacups with us.

To this day I can't help but smile when I read Psalm 16 and consider how the Lord assigned me my portion and my cup. The brew of life poured out by God conforms me to his heart. I've lived through crushing disappointments, broken vows and rampant sin. I've witnessed new life, revival and pure joy. All of it—the pleasure and the pain alike—placed within the bounds of God's hands, becomes a pleasant place, for I enter into his delightful inheritance.

ACT: *Whether it's a teacup, a journal, a piece of art or some other object, choose a symbolic reminder of God's great love for you and keep it close at hand.*

MARSHA CROCKETT

MONDAY *Transferring the Title*

> *He who began a good work in you will carry it on to completion*
> *until the day of Christ Jesus.*

PHILIPPIANS 1:6

Before I surrendered my life to the Lord, I kicked a well-meaning but bumbling Christian out of my dorm room for trying to tell me I was sinful and separated from God. I wasn't sinful; I was a good person! Six months later, I realized how desperately empty my trying-to-be-good life really was, and I became a Christian in that very same room.

My heart became Christ's home because he wouldn't leave me alone. Everything I did over a six-month period proved me wrong about my own life. Trials, disappointments, getting caught in hypocrisy and not living up to my own expectations set me up to hear the promise of God that the Spirit of the once-dead-and-now-alive Jesus could come into my life and change everything. It's been thirty-four years and six months since I tossed that Christian out of my room. God was listening then, and the rest is my history!

JOURNAL: *Write down the story of your giving Jesus the title to your heart. Celebrate the history Jesus has written for you since then.*

ROBBIE CASTLEMAN

Deep Roots

> *Jesus knew that the Father had put all things under his power,*
> *and that he had come from God and was returning to God.*

JOHN 13:3

Jesus knew who he was. He had a firm sense of identity, was rooted in his Father. And his actions flowed from his identity. His "doing" was a natural result of his "being."

Do we find ourselves deeply rooted in Christ? Being deeply rooted in him prevents us from doing things in secret that interfere with our intimacy with him. If we are convinced that our lives are hidden with Christ, we are saved from gaining our identity from our accomplishments or other people's opinions about us. Knowing that we're connected to the Vine enables us to trust that we're not alone in fearful or unsettling situations. Being grafted into Christ means that we've been adopted, chosen to be a son or daughter. We belong. We are heirs. And so our "doing" can be a natural result of our "being."

A C T : *Take the day off from doing things for God. Instead, enjoy the experience of being part of God's family.*

CAROLYN CARNEY

No Longer My Own

If we live, we live to the Lord; and if we die, we die to the Lord.
So, whether we live or die, we belong to the Lord.

ROMANS 14:8

Recently my husband and I deeded our woods to our local park district to be a nature preserve forever. The paperwork did not change anything about the property. When I walk down into the wooded ravine behind our home, it looks the same. The soft earth smells as rich and rooty as before. Twigs snap and leaves crackle beneath my feet the same as ever. But something is different. I know that it is no longer mine. Never before have I walked in that woods without the feeling that it is mine. Now I can never wholly feel that way again.

When we put our trust in Christ, we do not get a physical overhaul. People still recognize us on the street. But we are changed. We can never again think of ourselves as our own people. Ownership has changed hands, and we belong to Christ.

JOURNAL: *What stands out for you in the idea that you are God's and not your own? Celebrate your owner.*

SANDY LARSEN

Put Your Whole Self In

I urge you . . . to offer your bodies as living sacrifices,
holy and pleasing to God.

ROMANS 12:1

Have you ever done the Hokey Pokey? It's that little song and dance in which we put certain body parts into the circle, shake them and then "turn ourselves about." It's an active and sometimes tiring little exercise that ends with the command, "Put your whole self in . . ." When I think of that song and dance, I'm reminded of Paul's instruction: "Offer your bodies as living sacrifices" (Romans 12:1). It's Paul's way of saying, "Put your whole self in."

Most of us understand the idea of giving an offering of money at church. There are plates and envelopes, and we put our money or our check in an envelope and drop it in the plate. But we can't put ourselves in an envelope. We can't climb into the plate when the usher comes by and say, "My offering to God today is myself." For most of us it would be easier to take out our checkbooks and double our offering than it would be to turn ourselves over to God.

REFLECT: *Think of ways you could give to God that are unlike how you've given to God before—picking up trash along the side of the road, or sending anonymous cards to people, telling them of God's love.*

RICK EZELL

The Deeds to Our Hearts

> *He anointed us, set his seal of ownership on us,*
> *and put his Spirit in our hearts as a deposit.*

2 CORINTHIANS 1:21-22

Going through my mother's safe deposit box, I found the original abstract for my grandparents' house, my mother's childhood home. It was a thick document dating back to before 1900. I was surprised that we still had it, because the house was sold over thirty years ago. When I inquired of the present owner, he said he had been told the abstract was lost. I believe that my mother simply could not bear to hand it over when the house was sold. I gave the abstract to the present owner, but not before I photocopied the whole thing for myself.

Christ is the rightful owner of our bodies and souls. His claim to ownership is not a paper document in a safe deposit box but the Holy Spirit in our hearts.

ACT: *Make a "deed" to symbolize that you belong to Christ. Place it somewhere that will remind you that Christ is your Lord.*

SANDY LARSEN

The Waiting Game

I wait for the LORD, my soul waits, and in his word I put my hope.

PSALM 130:5

Trapeze artists know that there is a special relationship between the flyer and the catcher. As the flyer is swinging high above the crowd, the moment comes when he lets go of the trapeze, when he is suspended in nothingness. It is too late to reach back for the trapeze, but it is too soon to be grasped by the one who will catch him. He cannot accelerate the catch. In that moment, his job is to be as still and as motionless as he can. He must wait in absolute trust that the catcher will catch him. His job is not to flail about in anxiety. In fact, if he does, it could kill him. His job is to be still. To wait.

Waiting on God is the in-between time, the time of panic when our lives seem frozen in midair for a month, a year, a decade. During those times we must patiently trust in God, believing that he will always catch us.

JOURNAL: *Recall a feeling of in-betweenness. Is it hard to be still as you wait for God to bring you safely across? What helps you to wait in confidence?*

RICK EZELL

Advent

M O N D A Y

Advent Waiting

> *In this hope we were saved. But hope that is seen is no hope at all. . . .*
> *If we hope for what we do not yet have, we wait for it patiently.*

ROMANS 8:24-25

Advent is a season of waiting and anticipation. As Christmas approaches, remember those who longed for the Messiah: aged Simeon who blessed the baby Jesus, the eastern magi who sky-watched for years, old Elizabeth and young Mary, both expectant. And finally, the long-expected came!

Now *we* wait. He will come again, not as a vulnerable baby but as a victorious king, bringing full salvation and universal *shalom* to the world. We wait, but not passively. We do our best to straighten our lives and walk rightly. We pray—and work—for his kingdom to come everywhere. We wait, despite our inward groans of failure and pain and disappointment, because, whatever our present suffering, it will not compare with the glory to be revealed. It is something worth waiting for!

REFLECT: *What are your deepest longings? This advent season, renew your hopeful waiting for God to give you all he has promised.*

BOBBY GROSS

Making Your Heart a Home

The LORD had said to Abram,
"Leave your country, your people and your father's household
and go to the land I will show you."

GENESIS 12:1

When I visited Antigua, Guatemala, my eyes were drawn to the doors in the architecture. Usually made of wood, they bore intricate carvings and were painted bright colors, each one unique, perhaps hinting at the personalities living behind them.

The Antiguan doors spoke to me about my journey with Christ and the doorways throughout my life. Will I choose to open a door and walk through or pass up the opportunity? Where will a door lead and how will my life be affected?

Abram undoubtedly faced these questions as he crossed miles of desert en route to an unknown land. Walking through a door takes risk and courage because we don't know what will be on the other side. It's unfamiliar territory. The only thing that is familiar is God's unchanging hand holding ours.

PRAY: *Are you facing a door today? Ask God in faith to lead you through it.*

CAROLYN CARNEY

The Study

> *So do not be ashamed to testify about our Lord,*
> *or ashamed of me his prisoner. . . .*
> *Our Savior, Christ Jesus, . . . has destroyed death and has brought life*
> *and immortality to light through the gospel.*

2 TIMOTHY 1:8, 10

Death and bereavement can bring bitter sorrow. But these verses tell us that death itself has been overthrown. As the apostle Paul was languishing in some dark, dank dungeon in Rome, from which there was to be no escape but death, his thoughts turned to what it means to die in Christ. He was in chains, suffering acutely from the loneliness, boredom and cold of prison life. Is it not truly wonderful that, although Paul's body was confined within the narrow limits of an underground cell, his heart and mind could soar into eternity?

REFLECT: *If you knew you were going to die in a month, what do you hope would occupy your mind?*

JOHN STOTT

Resident Truth

Let the word of Christ dwell in you richly.

COLOSSIANS 3:16

We've lived in our home for twelve years. We've settled in. We know every corner, every creaky stair. We know what is in good shape (the roof) and what will probably need to be replaced in the next year or so (the furnace). We feel at home in this house—comfortable, secure, at rest.

That's the image Paul uses to describe how God's Word should fit into our hearts. The word *dwell* means to settle into a home, to take up permanent residence. Christians are called to grow in their understanding of the Word, and then we are to let that Word settle in. God's truth should feel at home in our hearts. It's not a visitor or an intruder but a permanent resident, the owner of the home.

PRAY: *Spirit of God, make my heart a peaceful home for God's truth.*

DOUGLAS CONNELLY

Confess your sins to each other and pray for each other so that you may be healed.

JAMES 5:16

Visionaries invest considerable time looking out the window, eagerly seeking to discern the fresh winds of the Spirit. This is profitable. But wise Christ-followers look not only to the horizon; they also gaze into the mirror of the soul, where the Spirit performs his hidden, transforming work.

It is disconcerting, however, to view our inner world, a place filled with sinful longings, petty complaints and selfish preoccupations. Our temptation is to substitute what Dallas Willard calls "sin management" for true repentance and spiritual transformation. We tend to create an inflated view of ourselves, ignoring the depth of our own brokenness and wrongdoing.

Yet self-examination, while necessary, has its limits. We need the mirror of community. Jean Vanier writes, "Community is the place where our limitations, our fears and egoism are revealed to us." Looking out the window is exhilarating. Looking in the mirror of truth is humiliating—unless we do it *together*, in the grace-filled, boundless love of Christ. It is there that we can truly change.

A C T : *If you don't already have one, take steps toward finding a confidential and safe spiritual friendship.*

BILL DONAHUE

Working for Redemption

Whatever you do, work at it with all your heart,
as working for the Lord.

COLOSSIANS 3:23

What is the purpose of having a job? Certainly it helps to put food on the table. But working at a job also demonstrates that we are made in the image of God. We can glorify him in our work.

Recently, a friend of mine declared that he was leaving the field of business for social work, because "business people are only out for a buck, and social workers serve people's needs." The "godly" choice was obvious to him. But social work is only one field among many—including business—that God can use toward his purposes. Engineering helps to bring clean water to rural areas. Entrepreneurs generate jobs that provide income to the unemployed. Any job has the capacity to serve God's redemptive purpose; what's most important is the willingness of the worker to work toward that purpose.

REFLECT: *What are some ways you could serve God's redemptive purposes through your work?*

CAROLYN CARNEY

MONDAY

Why, you do not even know what will happen tomorrow. What is your life?
You are a mist that appears for a little while and then vanishes.

JAMES 4:14

The one certainty in life is that life is uncertain. One day there are two huge towers in the New York skyline, and the next day they are gone. One day a president's approval rating is firmly ensconced in the upper percentages, and the next day he can't get elected. One day a person goes off to work, refusing to take a vacation with his family because the company could never get along without him, and the next day he has a heart attack and dies.

Life is uncertain. But uncertain is not the same as hopeless. Oh, no. For although all around us things may change, we who belong to the Lord rest securely in the hands of the one who is unchangeable: "Jesus Christ is the same yesterday and today and forever" (Hebrews 13:8).

JOURNAL: *What is it that you fear the most? Take some time now to commit that fear to your unchanging Lord.*

KAY MARSHALL STROM

Patience

> *"I know that . . . after my skin has been destroyed,*
> *yet in my flesh I will see God."*
>
> J O B   1 9 : 2 5 - 2 6

The patience of Job." People who use that phrase haven't read the story very carefully. Job was hurt and confused. He cursed the day he was born. He angrily chided and railed at God as he proclaimed his innocence. And he was not patient about it.

Not that I blame him. He was destitute, sick and in great pain, and he was grieving the deaths of his children. Then along came his friends. Instead of comforting him, they accused him of sin, preached to him and warned him to repent.

And so, in chapter 19, Job poured out a torrent of anger toward God. Yet in the midst of his anger and despair, Job remembered who he was talking to. Job was waiting—even though he was not patient. He knew the time would come when he would see God. And when that time came, all his suffering would be forgotten.

P R A Y : *If you are angry at God, go ahead and tell him. Then write down a statement that will remind you of who God really is.*

KAY MARSHALL STROM

The Workroom

I delight greatly in the LORD; my soul rejoices in my God.

ISAIAH 61:10

The phone connection was poor. I heard my friend say, "I've been going to choir practice and I feel so much better!" I was glad; it was the first I'd heard her say anything about going to church. Then she started talking about how her back and neck weren't so stiff anymore, and I realized she hadn't said "choir practice." She had said "chiropractor."

I was not surprised that a person would feel good about going to choir practice. Worship and fellowship with the people of God should bring us a holy pleasure. If church has become a drag for you, are you trying to do things outside the areas of your gifts or without a servant attitude? Service can be hard work and still be done joyfully.

R E F L E C T : *What church activities bring you the most joy, and why? Which activities feel like a chore? How can you regain your joy in those areas?*

SANDY LARSEN

THURSDAY *Believing the Unseen*

We fix our eyes not on what is seen, but on what is unseen.

2 CORINTHIANS 4:18

I had ordered a Bradford pear tree from a nursery. I received a stick with a ball of roots.

I was skeptical—*Could a whole tree really be in here?*—but I got to work and planted it. Taking off my gardening gloves, I shook my head and said, "Now, that's a stick!"

The weeks went by and I forgot about my little stick—until one day when I walked past it and there, to my surprise, were four small, green shoots. It worked! There was something going on beneath the ground that I could not see or control, and a living tree was being birthed in my very own backyard.

In life there is an unseen reality that lies just below the surface of the tangible, waiting to be embraced. Thomas Merton said, "The man who waits to see clearly, before he will believe, never starts on the journey."

REFLECT: *Recall a recent disappointment or a current anxiety. Ask God to birth something redemptive out of it.*

CAROLYN CARNEY

FRIDAY   *The Recreation Room*

God keeps him occupied with gladness of heart.

ECCLESIASTES 5:20

I don't like sports. There, I said it. And yet, the more I talk to people who like sports—like watching games on television, like playing in pick-up games at the gym—the more I'm impressed with the contribution sports makes to their lives. People recall stories of significant games in great detail, from the pumping of their heart as they ran downfield, to the temperature of their nacho cheese sauce as they absorbed the action on-screen.

We express ourselves in part through our pursuit of leisure. Leisure, whether action-packed or quiet and relaxed, leads to the exhilaration of a given moment, the unbridled joy that sustains us during times when hard work must be done. We remember such times of exhilaration because, as Jesus suggested, life to the full is life at its most memorable.

JOURNAL: *Revisit an old sports memory. What made it enjoyable? How can your downtime this weekend contribute to your soul's health?*

DAVID A. ZIMMERMAN

The Rhythms of the Year

*"These are the LORD's appointed feasts,
the sacred assemblies you are to proclaim at their appointed times."*

LEVITICUS 23:4

God provides rhythms for our lives: wakefulness and sleep each day, work and rest each week. One way he shaped the Jews into a "holy nation" was by giving them an annual pattern of festivals. The early Christians celebrated the Feasts of the Nativity (Christmas) and the Resurrection (Easter). Advent and Lent were later added as periods of preparation, and still later came the Feasts (and seasons) of Epiphany and Pentecost.

My worship life is set within an annual cycle that reflects the story of Christ: birth, life, death, resurrection, ascension and empowerment. My devotions, regular in time and place, become enriched by the dynamic rhythms of anticipation and celebration, of repentance and grace, of longing and joy. Such patterns remind us that our lives are shaped by his life, our stories by his story.

REFLECT: *How might the Christian calendar provide a rhythm to your spiritual life in the coming year?*

BOBBY GROSS

M O N D A Y

The Bedroom

> *His mouth is sweetness itself; he is altogether lovely.*
> *This is my lover, this is my friend.*
>
> SONG OF SONGS 5:16

One of the sweetest things about my husband is that he freely showers me with kind and loving words of intimate praise. To him, I really am beautiful! It's hard to believe that at first I was actually embarrassed by his words.

Why is it that so many Christians act as though passionate words of love between husband and wife are inappropriate? Evidently they have not read the Song of Solomon. This love poem overflows with expressions of passion and romantic joy. "Beloved"—whoever she might have been—enjoyed Solomon's attentions, and she drew strength from his love. With fullest feeling she responded by exclaiming, "My lover, my friend!"

ACT: *Express your love and affection for a loved one today. Be creative.*

KAY MARSHALL STROM

TUESDAY   *Two Become One*

> *If two lie down together, they will keep warm.*
> *But how can one keep warm alone?*

ECCLESIASTES 4:11

When God looked at Adam, his crowning creation, he declared, "It is not good for the man to be alone. I will make a helper suitable for him" (Genesis 2:18). And that's just what he did. He made a woman—Eve. Further along, in Genesis 2:24, we read, "For this reason a man will leave his father and mother and be united to his wife, and they will become one flesh."

A husband and wife are to leave the custody of their parents and together begin a new family, establishing an inseparable union with each other. It was a wonderful plan. Over time, so much interconnectedness occurs in a good marriage that it becomes difficult to think of one partner without thinking of the other. What a wonderful picture of God and his beloved—the church!

JOURNAL: *How does the idea of marriage shape your interaction with God? with the church?*

KAY MARSHALL STROM

The Hall Closet

> *"Blessed are the poor in spirit, for theirs is the kingdom of heaven.*
> *Blessed are those who mourn, for they will be comforted."*

MATTHEW 5:3-4

Some Christians think that they must wear a perpetual grin and be continuously boisterous and bubbly. However, the Christian life, according to Jesus, is not all joy and laughter. The truth is that there are such things as Christian tears, and too few of us ever weep them. As the second Beatitude teaches, sorrow can be the source of blessing.

Confession, the topic of the first Beatitude, is our acknowledgment that we are spiritually poor. Contrition, the topic of the second Beatitude, is to mourn and grieve over our sin. One might almost translate the second Beatitude "happy are the unhappy" in order to draw attention to the startling paradox it contains. It is not the sorrow of bereavement to which this beatitude refers, but the sorrow of repentance.

Those who bewail their own sinfulness will be comforted by the only comfort that can relieve their distress, namely, the free forgiveness of God.

PRAY: *Confess your sins to God. Allow Christ to speak peace and comfort to you.*

JOHN STOTT

Cleaning Up

*Let us throw off everything that hinders
and the sin that so easily entangles.*

HEBREWS 12:1

Our eighteen-year-old tackled the bathroom closet one day in my absence. I came home to organized, accessible storage. But after my initial delight, my collector's fears surfaced. "What did you throw away? Did you pitch anything we need?"

"No, Mom, trust me. I didn't toss anything we need."

But how could she know what we need? I pawed through the neatly tied bags of discards before they went to the garbage. A nearly empty shampoo bottle, some dribs of lotion—I could use those; it would save us a few cents. Soon I'd salvaged quite a haul.

I'm like this with God too. "Muzzle my mouth around my children more, so I can listen to them better? Sometimes I have appropriate words, God." "Initiate forgiveness? God, it wasn't my fault . . ."

Collecting sure clutters things up, both in the home and in my heart. Next time we clean out, I'm taking the stuff right to the trash—and leaving it there.

REFLECT: *What is God asking you to pitch? Do it now!*

JANE RUBIETTA

The Family Room

"Come, follow me . . . and I will make you fishers of men."

MATTHEW 4:19

I am my father's daughter. He was a fisherman, and when I was a little girl he would say to my sister and me, "Follow me, and I will make you fishers of fish!" So we followed him, because we loved him, and he taught us his trade.

Later, in college, the girl who led me to the Lord did not know that my father was a fisherman, but Matthew 4:19 is the first Scripture we read after I came to Christ. I learned that when Jesus called his disciples to follow him they were not all fishermen by trade, but every follower of Jesus needed to become a fisher of men.

As soon as I returned home from college, I gathered my friends together for a party in my parents' home and "went fishing"! Even today, there is no greater joy, for my heavenly Father is a fisherman, and I am my Father's daughter!

JOURNAL: *What scares you about fishing for people? Who would you like to see landed in God's fishing boat?*

JILL BRISCOE

What Is Your Name?

The disciples were called Christians first at Antioch.

ACTS 11:26

It's an old story. A young officer in the army of Alexander the Great was ushered before the great general on charges of actions unbecoming of an officer. The charges were read and the officer presented his defense. Before executing the sentence, Alexander asked the young officer's name.

"Alexander," the young officer said softly.

"Alexander?" the general questioned. With a look of fury, he said to the young officer with the same name as his, "Either change your conduct or change your name."

In the end, we wear the name *Christian* not because of what we are or who we are or where we are, but because of *whose* we are. It is not that we chose the name *Christian* but that we are given that name as we yield ourselves totally to Jesus Christ. Our goals, our ambitions, our talents, our desires are all abandoned. Like the believers at Antioch, we bear the name of Jesus in word and deed all the time.

REFLECT: *How can you wear the name* Christian *today in a way that is deserving of that designation?*

RICK EZELL

M O N D A Y

The Nativity of Our Lord

*"The rising sun will come to us from heaven to shine on those living in darkness
and in the shadow of death, to guide our feet into the path of peace."*

LUKE 1:78-79

It's at Christmastime that our homes most explicitly display the presence of
Christ· a bright tree in the living room, a crèche and candles on the den man-
tle, festive food at the dining table. But we all know the irony of Jesus being
crowded from our hearts in the bustle and buying of Yuletide.

Zechariah's prophecy boldfaces the true themes of this day: *light* cracking
our world's despairing horizon, *life* reversing our suffering and death, and a
profound vision of *peace* to animate our choices. Christmas Day! We turn from
our frenetic, grasping preoccupations and, instead, joyfully open our hearts
and hands.

Our lives may seem like dark and dingy stables, but when we open ourselves to Jesus, like a door to the dawn, he enters to take up residence, bringing
life and peace to us and to all around us.

REFLECT: *How can your traditional Christmas practices more fully celebrate
the light and life and peace that mark the season?*

BOBBY GROSS

The Back Porch

> *"Teacher, don't you care if we drown?"...*
> *they were terrified and asked each other, "Who is this?"*

MARK 4:38-41

Someone pointed out to me once that it's only when the disciples get displaced—knocked out of their familiar surroundings—that they ask the question, "Who is this?" It takes them a long time to consider that Jesus might be more than a teacher.

It's easy to stay inside, in our comfortable home with our comfortable stuff and familiar patterns. Sometimes it's even important to do that, for the sake of rest and in order to give our attention to what's going on inside us. But we ought to get out onto the porch regularly, too, to take in the sights and smells and sounds of all else going on in the world around us. It is often when we run into something we can't interpret or don't understand that Jesus' character becomes clear to us.

PRAY: *Jesus, help me trust you today. Help me to step beyond my own world to encounter the world as you do.*

ALISON SIEWERT

> *A woman . . . learned that Jesus was eating at the Pharisee's house*
> *[and] brought an alabaster jar of perfume.*
>
> L U K E   7 : 3 7

In sea adventures those who survive a sinking ship often gather up floating debris and piece together some makeshift raft. Such a raft takes you someplace that you couldn't have gone without it, someplace you may never have thought to go otherwise.

The alabaster jar in Luke 7:37 represents the brokenness of a woman's past life. She sneaks into the Pharisee's house, overwhelmed with gratitude for what Jesus has done for her. What follows is undoubtedly one of the most intimate portraits in the Gospels. The woman empties her broken vessel, devoting her priceless perfume to Jesus, and experiences a fellowship with God she never thought imaginable.

We usually want to be as far away from our brokenness as we can possibly get. Tragedy hits and we want to go the other way. But our brokenness can be the vehicle to experiencing deeper aspects of a trust relationship with God.

JOURNAL: *What brokenness in your life would you rather forget? What would Jesus do with it if you poured it at his feet?*

CAROLYN CARNEY

I remember the days of long ago;
I meditate on all your works and consider what your hands have done.

PSALM 143:5

We have made many winter trips across Michigan's remote Upper Peninsula, but one trip dominates my memories. Shortly before Christmas we set out on a twelve-hour drive. Late in the afternoon an oncoming truck forced us to run off the road into a snowdrift. We got back on the road, but as evening came on, our headlights began to dim. The fan belt had gotten wet and was slipping, so the alternator was not keeping the battery charged. Light snow became heavy and slowed us to a crawl. To save the engine, Dale switched to parking lights only. We eventually reached our destination, though our lights faded again before we got there.

When I talk about trips across the Upper Peninsula, I don't tell stories of the problem-free journeys. I tell the story of the snowdrift and the failing battery and the darkness. It does me good to remember how on that trip the Lord kept us safe and kept us going.

REFLECT: *Let your memories of God's works in the past encourage you in present difficulties.*

SANDY LARSEN

Transferring the Title

"I am the Lord's servant," Mary answered.
"May it be to me as you have said."

LUKE 1:38

Who can understand the rhyme or reason of God choosing to be confined in the womb of a young girl? Who can understand the rhyme or reason of a young girl choosing to be confined herself, receiving God into her body and changing her life forever?

No, I don't understand the incarnation, but I know God's choosing to come in the flesh is wrapped up in love. And Mary's response—"Let it be with me according to your word"—is not one of resignation but of devoted surrender.

A thoughtful person once told me that Mary was the first person to receive Christ. Her "yes" is an example for all of us. It is left to us to be like Mary, to say "yes" to Jesus coming into our lives, to be willing to be changed from this time and forever.

PRAY: *Ask God to give you faith like Mary.*

CAROLYN CARNEY

My Heart—Christ's Home

"Did I not tell you that if you believed, you would see the glory of God?"

JOHN 11:40

Jesus was always welcome and often returned with delight to the home of Mary, Martha and their brother, Lazarus. During the days of his final week in Jerusalem he encountered relentless opposition and antagonism from his enemies. In the evenings he returned to Bethany to be received in the home of his friends.

Consider what Jesus brought to that home: not only the joy of his companionship but an experience of his life and power. He promised them that if they would believe in him they would see the glory of God. They saw the glory of God in the raising to life of Lazarus upon Jesus' spoken word.

The same Lord is with us. These hearts of ours may be as true a home for Jesus Christ as was the house in which Mary, Martha and Lazarus received him so long ago.

REFLECT: *Think of your physical body as a structure with the walls of flesh and blood; the door, your power of choice. How can you welcome Jesus to settle down and be at home?*

ROBERT BOYD MUNGER

ACKNOWLEDGMENTS

The publisher gratefully acknowledges all the authors and church leaders who have contributed entries to this devotional book.

Ken Fong's entries are adapted from his book *Secure in God's Embrace* ©2003. Published by InterVarsity Press. Used by permission. *Pages 50, 122*

Ken Gire's entry is adapted from his book *The Divine Embrace* ©2003. Published by Tyndale House. Used by permission. *Page 100*

Ben Patterson's entries are adapted from his book *He Has Made Me Glad* ©2004. Published by InterVarsity Press (forthcoming). Used by permission. *Pages 37, 88, 111*

John Stott's entries are adapted from the following books:

The Message of 1 Timothy and Titus ©John R. W. Stott, 1996. Published by InterVarsity Press. Used by permission. *Page 65*

The Message of 2 Timothy ©John R. W. Stott 1973. Published by InterVarsity Press. Used by permission. *Page 307*

The Message of the Sermon on the Mount ©John R. W. Stott 1978. Published by InterVarsity Press. Used by permission. *Page 319*

Special thanks go to the freelance writers who helped create this book. Their contributions can be found using the index on pages 334-35.

Carolyn Carney is a missionary serving with InterVarsity Christian Fellowship/USA in South Africa.

Douglas Connelly is a pastor and the author of many books, including ten LifeGuide Bible studies and the book *Angels Around Us* (IVP).

Marsha Crockett is the author of several books, including *Dancing in the Desert* and *Weaving a Life of Prayer* (IVP).

Rick Ezell is a pastor and the author of *Defining Moments* and *Sightings of the Savior* (IVP).

Bobby Gross is a regional director for InterVarsity Christian Fellowship/USA, and a contributor to the book *Faith on the Edge* (IVP).

Sandy Larsen is the author, with her husband, of more than thirty books and Bible studies, including the Christian Classics Bible Studies *Dietrich Bonhoeffer, Jonathan Edwards* and *Teresa of Ávila* (IVP).

Jane Rubietta is the author of several books, including *Grace Points: Growth and Guidance in Times of Change* (IVP).

Alison Siewert is cofounder and director of the theater group ransomTHEdon-Key, and author of *Drama Team Handbook* and *Drama Team Sketchbook* (IVP).

Kay Marshall Strom is the author of more than thirty books, including *Daughters of Hope: Stories of Witness and Courage in the Face of Persecution* (IVP).

Devotions in this book are arranged by category and identified as "rooms" of the heart.

Making Your Heart a Home—Inviting Christ into our lives and experiencing the presence of the Holy Spirit. *Pages 9-14, 83-88, 157-62, 231-36, 306*

The Study—Recognizing the role of the mind in loving Christ. *Pages 15-20, 89-94, 163-68, 237-42, 307-8*

The Dining Room—Gaining control of worldly appetites and feasting on God's will. *Pages 21-26, 95-100, 169-74, 243-48, 309-10*

The Living Room—Going deep in our relationship with Christ through Bible study and prayer. *Pages 27-32, 101-6, 175-80, 249-54, 311-12*

The Workroom—Learning to use our spiritual gifts to serve others. *Pages 33-38, 107-12, 181-86, 255-60, 313-14*

The Recreation Room—Finding joy in making Christ a part of all of our relationships and activities. *Pages 39-44, 113-18, 187-92, 261-66, 315-16*

The Bedroom—Grasping God's involvement in our rest and his intent for our sexuality in all areas of life. *Pages 45-50, 119-24, 193-98, 267-72, 317-18*

INDEX OF FEASTS AND HOLIDAYS

Feasts and holidays are often not assigned to specific dates but rather acknowledged in relation to one another. Maundy Thursday, for example, is celebrated three days before Easter Sunday, while Pentecost is celebrated fifty days after Easter. We have placed devotions inspired by the following feast days and holidays near where they might normally fall in a calendar year. More information about the church calendar is available at <www.cyberfaith.com/calendar_index.html>.